Radical Recovery

12 Recovery Myths: The Addiction Survivor's Guide To The Twelve Steps

☥ ☥ ☥ ☥ ☥

KELLY

BALBOA PRESS
A DIVISION OF HAY HOUSE

Copyright © 2012 Kelly

All rights reserved. No part of this book may be used or reproduced by any means, graphic, electronic, or mechanical, including photocopying, recording, taping or by any information storage retrieval system without the written permission of the publisher except in the case of brief quotations embodied in critical articles and reviews.

Balboa Press books may be ordered through booksellers or by contacting:

Balboa Press
A Division of Hay House
1663 Liberty Drive
Bloomington, IN 47403
www.balboapress.com
1-(877) 407-4847

Because of the dynamic nature of the Internet, any web addresses or links contained in this book may have changed since publication and may no longer be valid. The views expressed in this work are solely those of the author and do not necessarily reflect the views of the publisher, and the publisher hereby disclaims any responsibility for them. The author of this book does not dispense medical advice or prescribe the use of any technique as a form of treatment for physical, emotional, or medical problems without the advice of a physician, either directly or indirectly. The intent of the author is only to offer information of a general nature to help you in your quest for emotional and spiritual well-being. In the event you use any of the information in this book for yourself, which is your constitutional right, the author and the publisher assume no responsibility for your actions.

Any people depicted in stock imagery provided by Thinkstock are models, and such images are being used for illustrative purposes only.

All rights reserved. No part of this book may be used or reproduced by any means, graphic, electronic, or mechanical, including photocopying, recording, taping or by any information storage retrieval system without the written permission of the publisher except in the case of brief quotations, embodied in critical articles and reviews.

The brief excerpts from Alcoholics Anonymous and Twelve Steps and Twelve Traditions reprinted with permission of Alcoholics Anonymous World Services, Inc. ("AAWS") Permission to reprint these excerpts does not mean that AAWS has reviewed or approved the contents of this publication, or that AAWS necessarily agrees with the views expressed herein. A.A. is a program of recovery from alcoholism only – use of these excerpts in connection with programs and activities which are patterned after A.A., but which address other problems, or in any other non A.A. context, does not imply otherwise.

ISBN: 978-1-4525-5711-3 (sc)
ISBN: 978-1-4525-5710-6 (e)
ISBN: 978-1-4525-6464-7 (hc)
Library of Congress Control Number: 2012922888
Printed in the United States of America
Balboa Press rev. date: 12/18/2012

This book is dedicated to:

My wife Mavis for her continuous support of my work as an addiction counselor, and her love and support in my writing this book.

My mother for her courage, resilience, wit, charm, and prayers. My father for his poetic genes and the lessons learned. My brothers and sister for their unconditional love.

Bill, Liz, Roger, and Mike Dandreo who helped me blaze new paths in treating addiction.

The editors: George Roberts, Larry Sullivan, and my wife Mavis who took the time to read and edit the book throughout its development.

Rich and Vivian Osborne and the many other parents who have lost children to this terminal disease.

WARNING

If you have been on the *Relapse Roller Coaster Ride* during the last several years, and you're not sure if you want to get off, then *you shouldn't read this book*.

One of the major side effects is **emotional sobriety**. You may get *SOBER*, in the fullest sense of the word; become well balanced, realistic, sensible, dignified, rational; not driven to extremes in emotion or thought.

If you are tired of being seduced by the promise of instant gratification and heavenly bliss that results in weeks, months, or years of living a hellish nightmare, then *you should read this book*.

Like Christopher Columbus, you may discover a new world; a world filled with intuition, imagination, creativity, and power.

"Are you willing to be sponged out, erased, canceled? Are you willing to be made nothing, dipped into oblivion? If not, you will never really change."
(D.H. Lawrence)

CONTENTS

PREFACE   xi
ALCOHOLICS AND ADDICTS THE RELUCTANT WARRIORS   1
Myth 1: ADDICTION IS A BAD HABIT NOT A DISEASE   15
Myth 2: I AM DIFFERENT FROM YOU   25
Myth 3: WE ARE POWERLESS OVER OUR ADDICTION   35
Myth 4: WE NEED A HIGHER POWER TO RECOVER   49
Myth 5: JUST DON'T PICK UP   63
Myth 6: ALCOHOL AND DRUGS MAKE OUR LIVES UN-MANAGEABLE   77
Myth 7: MEETING MAKERS MAKE IT   87
Myth 8: THERE IS NO CURE FOR ADDICTION   99
Myth 9: WE HAVE TO GET OUT OF THE DRIVER'S SEAT   111
Myth 10: THE STEPS SHOULD BE TAKEN IN ORDER   121
Myth 11: OUR DISEASE SPEAKS TO US   133
Myth 12: WILL-POWER IS USELESS WITH ADDICTION   141
SUMMARY   151

ABOUT THE AUTHOR

Kelly has more than thirty-five years of continuous sobriety and has been working in the recovery field as an addiction counselor for more than ten years. Kelly is certified in Addiction Counseling, Neuro Linguistic Programming, Trauma Therapy, Hypnosis, and is a Licensed HeartMath Provider. Kelly's innovative and therapeutic approaches for treating addiction have been adopted by treatment centers in the U.S. and Great Britain. In working as an interventionist, Kelly's approach has also met with success. The results achieved may mark a new era in treating addiction.

"At the beginning of the session, I felt skeptical. At the end of the session, I felt strong, powerful, good about myself. It gives me hope and courage." Richard P.

"At the beginning of the session, I was in physical pain. At the end of the session, the pain was gone." Kathy C.

"At the beginning of the session, I felt very anxious and pretty depressed. At the end of the session, I felt very relaxed, relieved, and worry free." Susan S.

"Of all the forms of therapy I have experienced, I would say this is one of the best of the best." Thomas M.

"At the beginning of the session, I felt angry, and ready to leave treatment. At the end of the session I was grateful for the good things I have in my life." Marie T.

"At the beginning of the session, I felt apprehensive At the end of the session, I felt calm, relaxed, and inspired. I felt like I can accomplish anything I set my mind to." Rob G.

"At the beginning of the session, I felt in pain and anxious. At the end of the session, I felt relaxed, hopeful, inspired, and empowered." Terry K.

"At the beginning of the session, I felt stressed, my muscles were cramping and all my joints were hurting. At the end of the session, I felt extremely relaxed, motivated and inspired to do good things."

"At the beginning of the session, I felt anxious. At the end of the session, I felt calm, relaxed, inspired, energized, and motivated." Kristen O.

"At the beginning of the session, I felt achy and very stressed. At the end of the session, I felt very relaxed, at ease, and peaceful." Lisa F.

PREFACE

Imagine a congregation of Palestinians, Jews, and Irish meeting at a convention.
What do they have in common?
They are all human beings.
But among these human beings there are many dramatic differences such as their religious beliefs, political views, and traditions.
Imagine a room filled with cases of liquor, large bundles of marijuana, cocaine, and heroin, along with large plastic bottles filled with Xanax, Vicodin, Percocet, and Oxycontin.
What do they have in common?
They are all drugs.
But there are some dramatic differences between them.
Alcohol is a legal drug.
Under current Federal Law, marijuana, cocaine, and heroin are illegal drugs.
Prescription drugs can only by obtained by visiting a doctor or drug dealer.
What we have to do to obtain them, the powerful effects they have on us, and the consequences of having them in our possession vary significantly.
That's why we have:
    www.chronicpainanonymous.org
    www.pillsanonymous.org
    www.aa.org, and
    www.na.org
One shoe doesn't fit all.
But we all have the same "primary" addiction.
We use these drugs to escape - from physical, mental, emotional, or spiritual pain.

To overcome the negative effects of our addiction to these drugs, we cannot be spectators.

We must become warriors.

A warrior is a man or woman who demonstrates great courage, commitment, discipline, endurance, persistence, resilience, patience, and humility.

"The strongest warriors are these two...
time and patience." (Leo Tolstoy)

I would add to this, repetition. That's how I learned my times table. That's how I learned how to grow spiritually, by *practicing* the spiritual principles of the Twelve Steps in my daily life. Throughout the book, some of the critical points we need to understand, if we want to become addiction survivors, are repeated. I did this deliberately. What is repeated again and again can become a natural part of us. What is seen, said, or done one time is seldom lasting.

Insanity comes in many forms, but there are two forms of insanity that are unique to addicts and alcoholics. It's important to know what they are.

One of the questions I have often asked myself is, why do so many of us who come into treatment glorify our alcohol and drug history?

Since there is no future in addiction, just a regrettable past that keeps repeating itself over and over again, I guess we really don't have anything else to talk about but the past.

But I also believe it's because we haven't found anything better, anything more stimulating or motivating than the highs we get from pills, alcohol, or drugs. Often, we are not looking for anything better, nor are we being *inspired* or *motivated* to seek anything better. It's pretty hard to get excited about using a doorknob or chair as a "Higher" Power.

Tapping into your imagination, can you imagine a butterfly telling a group of caterpillars that doorknobs have *magical powers* that can transform them into beautiful butterflies? Sounds silly, doesn't it?

For many of us, treatment is like a summer camp, a place we come to recuperate and relax, as long as we have cash, or insurance is willing to pay for it. In many cases, we are not accountable to ourselves or anyone else. Why?

Because until we are willing to do the work it takes to become an addiction survivor, we are classic examples of "self-will run riot."

Every time we pick up a pill, drink, or drug it's like playing Russian Roulette, and we all know people like Whitney Houston, (cocaine), Amy Winehouse, (alcohol), and Michael Jackson (prescription drugs), who lost the game.

Within our fellowship, it's said the *answers* are in the Big Book, (Alcoholics Anonymous), because it contains a great deal of wisdom. Let's see what wisdom we can find there regarding *why* we are not more accountable to ourselves or others.

"Most alcoholics have to be pretty badly mangled before they commence to solve their problem." (A.A. Page 43)

What motivated the original members of A.A. to solve their problem? They had a gift, the gift of desperation.

"We in our turn sought the same escape (from the slavery of alcoholism) with all the desperation of drowning men." (A.A. Page 28)

As a result of having this "gift", they had a very high recovery rate. Today, we have a very high relapse rate. Why is there such a radical difference?

While the causes of addiction can be complex, the answer may be simple.

To get the answer, you won't have to spend the next five years in therapy, or go through treatment ten more times. Here's some more wisdom from the Big Book.

"When our membership was small, we only dealt with *low bottom cases.* Many less desperate alcoholics tried A.A. but did not succeed because they could not make the admission of their hopelessness." *(Twelve Steps and Twelve Traditions - P 23)*

THE DILEMMA

A dilemma is a situation that requires making a choice between two equally undesirable alternatives. For the original members of A.A., the two equally undesirable alternatives they had to choose between were these:

"To be doomed to an alcoholic death or to live on a spiritual basis are not always easy alternatives to face." *(A.A. Page 44)*

In a broader sense, when we are confronted with some of the harsher realities of life such as loss of a job, death of a loved one, illness, divorce, custody battles, or feelings such as boredom, fear, anger, loneliness, resentments, anxiety, shame, guilt, or depression, the two equally undesirable alternatives we are faced with are coping or escaping. There is no third option. Both choices have some degree of pain associated with them.

ESCAPING

Alcohol and drugs provide a great escape.

They enable us to numb whatever mental, emotional, spiritual, or physical pain we may be feeling. But this *numbing* has a very negative side effect. It creates huge icebergs inside us.

Over time, these icebergs become like nagging toothaches.

We are always aware of their presence.

Until we find the courage to - go through the pain, they will never go away.

COPING

If we underestimate our own strength and resources, challenges that are well within our capacity to cope with, appear to be overwhelming.

This "underestimating" is something many of us began doing as children.

Recovery is a *process* which provides us with the tools and resources we need to gradually begin thawing the icebergs inside us; to develop the courage, strength, and commitment it takes to deal with the realities of life - without having to pick up a pill, drink, or drug.

THE PROBLEM

Our relationship with pills, alcohol, or drugs starts out as a habit.

Over time, it becomes an obsession and compulsion, which are both forms of Insanity.

We're doing something we don't want to do, and we can't stop doing it.

This is definitely one form of insanity that is unique to alcoholics and addicts.

Now you know why we have Step 2:

"Came to believe that a Power greater than ourselves could restore us to sanity."

BATTERIES

Imagine not being able to start your car in the morning because your battery is dead. You ask a neighbor to give you a jump start. Your neighbor agrees, but fails to tell you that his car battery is also dead.

It wouldn't take you long to figure out that your neighbor's car battery wasn't capable of providing you with the power you needed to get your car started.

If you decided to stay connected to this battery, hoping that some *magical event* would take place, this would be another form of insanity. Don't you agree?

When we arrive at the doors of A.A. or N.A. we are like a dead car battery. We **lack the power** to control the obsessive thoughts, compulsive feelings, and physical cravings that keep us trapped in the slavery of addiction.

We need to *connect* with a source of power that can provide us with the strength we need to tame the destructive forces that create so much pain and suffering in our lives, and the lives of those we love. Are you now ready to do that, connect with a source of Power than can free you from the slavery of addiction, or do you want to continue playing Russian Roulette?

I am going to use the word "Battery" instead of "Higher Power" to explore the options available to us. It's been said that love is the most powerful force in the universe. Think about the love you have for your spouse, partner, children, family, or friends. Surely, this is a Battery you can connect to!

But it's a dead Battery.

How many times have you said to yourself or those you love, "I am done. I'll never drink or use drugs again." A hundred times? A thousand times?

We need to *seek* and *find* something more powerful than love. Wouldn't you agree?

After much trial and error, the original members of A.A. learned to tell the difference between a live Battery and a dead Battery. It was pretty simple.

When they used Batteries that had power, they got sober.

When they used Batteries that didn't have power, they got drunk.

They identified three Batteries that enabled them to stop drinking and using drugs.
1. *God - as each of them understood Him.* This Battery made it possible for people of all faiths, Jews, Catholics, Protestants, Buddhists, Muslims, Hindu's etc., to embrace the spiritual principles in the Twelve Steps.
2. *Nature, a Creative Intelligence, Great Reality, or Spirit of the Universe.* This Battery made it possible for anyone who wasn't, or didn't want to be, part of any organized religion to join the Fellowship. Their belief, that there was some Force *greater than themselves*, made it easy for them to connect with this Battery.
3. *The A.A. Group.* For those who didn't believe in God, or doubted the existence of God, the A.A. group was the Battery they were able to connect with.

What kind of "power" did the group provide?

The power of unity, endurance, strength, support, tolerance, and unconditional love. to start

Wouldn't you agree that *any* alcoholic or drug addict who wants to get clean and sober should be able to connect with at least one of these three Batteries?

By believing in the power of God, a *Force* greater than themselves, or the group, the original members of A.A. went down a path that enabled them to accomplish the goal they set out to achieve, and that was - victory over alcohol.

"The problem has been removed. It does not exist for us." (A.A. Page 85)

There are several obvious reasons why we have a very high relapse rate.

One, is that somewhere between 1935, when A.A. was founded, and today, as a Fellowship, *we have lost the ability to tell the difference between a dead Battery and a live Battery.*

Let's start with love.

We need to *seek* and *find* something more powerful than love. Doesn't your experience confirm this fact?

Does a doorknob have more power than the love you have for your spouse, partner, children, friends, or family?

How about a chair?

What about a salt shaker?
Maybe a pencil?
Have you considered a shoe box?
And people wonder why we keep relapsing; why we don't "get it."

Perhaps the reason we don't "get it," is because, in many cases, "it" is not being offered to us.

Members of the Fellowship shouldn't be afraid to ask us:

"If you want what we have, are you willing to go to any lengths to get it?"

The reason for asking this question is important because if we don't want what they have, then they won't have to worry about whether or not we will get it.

What is the "it" that is not being offered to us?

THE TRUTH

What is the *truth* about addiction?

The sublime message passed on to us by the original members of A.A. was this:

"*You may be suffering from an illness which only a spiritual experience will conquer.*" (A.A. P 44)

This *sublime* message has been reduced to the *ridiculous* because at many meetings we are told that we can solve our problem by just not picking up a pill, drink, or drug.

If we had the *power* to "just not pick up," then obviously:

We wouldn't keep relapsing.

We wouldn't keep showing up at treatment centers, and we certainly wouldn't need to be a member of a Twelve Step program.

Isn't that right?

Try "just not picking up" the next time you want to smoke a cigarette. See how this solution works for you.

Would you be offended if, upon attending your first meeting, I asked you this question:

"If I could show you how to connect with a Power deep *inside* you that is *much more powerful* than your addiction, *much more powerful* than the obsessive thoughts, compulsive feelings, and physical cravings that create so much pain and suffering in your life, would you be interested?"

Would you say, "No, I am not interested."

Many members of A.A. treat the book, Alcoholics Anonymous, with the same reverence that people treat the Bible. A whole chapter of the book, *Working With Others*, provides guidance and direction on how to help newcomers. But the guidance and direction provided there is, in many groups, completely ignored. For example, it states:

"Stress the spiritual feature freely. If the man be agnostic or atheist, make it emphatic that *he does not have to agree with your perception of God.* He can choose any conception (of God) that he likes, provided it makes sense to him." *(A.A. Page 93)*

At many meetings the spiritual feature is buried, hidden, diluted, or distorted.

There's nothing spiritual about using inanimate objects such as a shoebox or a roll of toilet paper as a "Higher" Power.

They can't think, feel, or act which means - they are powers **less** than ourselves; not **greater** than ourselves.

To better appreciate the insanity of this common practice, here's how the dictionary defines the word INANIMATE:

"Dull, dead, lifeless, spiritless, something which **lacks the power** or force of living things."

The U.S. Marines and Navy Seals are not for everyone. Neither are the Twelve Steps.

But the U.S. Marines and Navy Seals aren't ashamed of what they represent.

Every Marine and Navy Seal is keenly aware of the courage, commitment, persistence, and endurance it takes to become part of that band of brothers.

They don't deny or attempt to hide "what it takes" to be a member of their team.

"What does it take" to become a member of a Fellowship that can help us recover from an illness which only a spiritual experience may conquer?

The answer found by Bill Wilson and millions of other alcoholics and addicts is this:

"It was only a matter of being willing to believe in a Power greater than myself. Nothing more was required of me to make my beginning." (A.A. Page 12)

If for some reason a newcomer is not interested in the *spiritual solution* offered by our Fellowship, here's some more wisdom from the Big Book:

"If he thinks he can do the job in some other way, or prefers some other spiritual approach, encourage him to follow his own conscience. We have no monopoly on God; we simply have an approach that worked with us." *(A.A. Page 95)*

Rational Recovery and SMART Recovery are two of many approaches to recovery that do not have a spiritual component.

So, if the spiritual solution does not appeal to someone, they have other options.

But perhaps it wouldn't be necessary for them to go that route if common sense prevailed, and members of the Fellowship suggested that they use the group as a Higher Power because the group actually has power.

Instead, at many meetings, the solution often presented is a *myth,* which the dictionary defines as:

"*An imaginary or fictitious thing or person, an unproved or false collective belief.*"

The unproved - false collective belief - often presented is that dead batteries: chairs, empty soda cans, doorknobs, salt shakers, and shoe boxes can provide us with the Power we need to recover from a disease that is *cunning, baffling, and powerful;* a disease, which, when it is left untreated, is terminal.

Sounds silly, doesn't it?

THE SECOND FORM OF INSANITY UNIQUE TO ALCOHOLICS AND ADDICTS

You agreed that it would be insane to stay connected to a dead battery if you wanted to get your car started.

Then, you would also have to agree that it's insane to believe that inanimate objects, which - lack the power or force of living things - can provide you with the Power you need to have a *spiritual experience* that can transform your cravings for pills, alcohol, or drugs into a craving for freedom, integrity, honesty, peace, and humility.

If you were diagnosed with cancer, can you imagine anyone at the American Cancer Society telling you that doorknobs and empty shoe boxes have "magical powers" that can cure cancer and other terminal diseases?

Because our brains are fried, or because we are in so much pain when we come into recovery, many of us take advice from people who we think are *supposedly* more sane than we are.

We connect to these dead batteries.

We buy into the myth.

As a consequence:

- We keep relapsing.
- We keep coming back to treatment, and
- We keep dying.

The Twelve Steps were designed to *restore* us to sanity, not *add* to the insanity in our lives.

My primary goal in writing this book is to not only shed light on the recovery myths that may be keeping you stuck on the *Relapse Roller Coaster Ride,* but to inspire, motivate, and empower you; to make you *aware* that:

You are *much more powerful* than your addiction.

You are *much more powerful* than the obsessive thoughts, compulsive feelings, and physical cravings that are the **sources** of all the unmanageability and suffering in your life.

INTRODUCTION

ALCOHOLICS AND ADDICTS THE RELUCTANT WARRIORS

"Know well what leads you forward and what holds you back, and choose the path that leads to wisdom." (The Buddha)

MARTIAL ARTS AND THE TWELVE Steps have much in common. To become a warrior or an addiction survivor requires courage, commitment, discipline, persistence, and endurance. It requires us to become more aware of the darkness in our lives – without being paralyzed by it.

This can be painful, like natural childbirth, because we no longer have our anesthetic, our drug of choice, to numb the pain that comes with transforming the darkness into light.

Just as a warrior is a protector of ideals, principles, and honor, the spiritual principles in the Twelve Steps guide us down a similar path. A warrior seeks to be both noble and heroic, essential qualities we need to develop as we begin the process of transforming our cravings for pills, alcohol, or drugs into cravings for courage, freedom, honesty, peace, and humility.

The warrior, like us, understands that the most formidable obstacle he will ever face during his life is his own self.

In following the path of the warrior, or the path of the Twelve Steps, we become conscious and aware of the good, bad, beautiful, and ugly parts of ourselves.

With this comes a *commitment* to conquer the flaws in our character that stand in the way of becoming noble and heroic: fear, anger, guilt, shame, resentment, lust, self-pity, arrogance, self-centeredness, and greed.

Learning how to overcome these powerful forces is the *true nature of victory* for alcoholics, addicts, and warriors.

In studying the history thousands of cultures Joseph Campbell found that all heroes and heroines go through the same process as alcoholics and addicts. They encounter a big problem. They want to ignore or deny the fact that they have a big problem. But they finally come to a fork in a road where ignoring or denying the problem is no longer an option. If they don't act, they will be forced to endure a great deal of suffering and pain, or die.

Before I came to the fork in the road where I finally had to make a choice, I was blind to the fact that I had a problem with alcohol and drugs.

I had an insomnia problem. Alcohol solved that problem.

I had a depression problem. The highs and numbing effects of drugs solved that problem.

I had an insanity problem, which was certainly preferable to having an alcohol or drug problem. I thought I could solve that problem by having a psychiatrist lock me up in a mental institution and throw the key away because *I didn't want to deal with reality any more.*

The insanity problem brought me to the fork in the road where I only had two options, take action or die. Taking action meant I would have to let go of all my crutches and begin a journey without knowing how it would end. This required courage.

The original members of A.A. had the courage and insight of a warrior. They understood that, *"Self, manifested in various ways was what defeated us (not a substance.)" (A.A. Page 62)*

To overcome the defects of character that created so much pain and suffering in their lives, and the lives of those they loved, the original members of A.A. set two noble and heroic goals.

One: "We would go to any lengths for **victory** over alcohol." *(A.A. Page 76)*

Two: "We decided to go to any lengths to **find** a spiritual experience." *(A.A. Page 79)*

How does one find? One seeks!

This summarizes our purpose for being a member of a Twelve Step program: **Spiritual Growth, and Character Development.**

Is this why you are a member of a Twelve Step program or have you bought into the myth that you can achieve victory over your addiction by just changing your behavior - not drinking or using drugs and going to meetings.

The "victory" sought by the original members of A.A. wasn't over a substance. They understood *what it takes* to become an addiction survivor. Before conquering their addiction, they knew they first had to tame the obsessive thoughts, compulsive feelings, and physical cravings that kept them trapped in a cycle of chronic relapses.

Many religions depict warriors in their imagery. These images are not symbols for brutality. Rather, they are symbols of the persistence, endurance, fortitude, and a commitment it takes to overcome the bad and ugly parts of ourselves and develop core values such as: honesty, fearlessness, humility, love, forgiveness, joy, patience, gentleness, and compassion.

As we go through the process of developing these core values, our attitude begins to change.

With this change in attitude, we begin to measure our progress by different standards.

Am I more honest?

Is my thinking sounder?

Can I remain calm when provoked?

Am I free from the conditioned responses of anger, fear, jealousy, and greed?

Have I stopped judging people who look, think, or feel differently than I do?

Let's pause here and ask this question:

Is a spiritual experience *really* necessary?

The answer is "No!"

Not for most people.

However, as stated earlier, if you are an alcoholic or addict:

"You may be suffering from an illness which only a spiritual experience will conquer." (A.A. P 44)

It's interesting to note that, in 1939, when the book *Alcoholics Anonymous* was published, this is how the medical profession viewed alcoholics:

"Among physicians, the general opinion seems to be that most chronic alcoholics are doomed." (A.A. Page xxx)

This tells us *why* the original members of A.A. were willing to go to any lengths to find a spiritual experience.

Today, research studies indicate that we have a relapse rate that falls somewhere between 80 and 90 percent. That being said, it might be in your best interest to develop the same willingness the original members of A.A. had to *seek and find* a spiritual experience. How can you do this?

The message is clear and simple.

The original members of A.A. **found** a spiritual experience as a **result** of immersing themselves in the Steps of our program.

Are you willing to immerse yourself in the Twelve Steps, and grab hold of them the way someone who is drowning grabs hold of a life preserver?

Are you willing to *commit* to getting a sponsor who will take you through all Twelve Steps so you can gain access to the Power you need to become an addiction survivor?

In martial arts, students start out equally.

If they are attacked, they automatically defend themselves. No thought is required.

As the students learn more techniques, they move to the next level, from unskilled to skillful.

They become more effective as their skills increase, but the emphasis on the techniques makes their movements artificial and unnatural.

After years of consistent practice, the students become one with their techniques. Their moves become automatic. They execute them perfectly, without thinking. They complete a circle which brings them back to natural state. But there is a big difference! They are now *skillful warriors,* performing at a much higher level than before.

This is similar to the path we follow as we begin to practice the spiritual principles of the Twelve Steps *as a way of life.*

SOBER

Our ultimate goal as members of a Twelve Step program is to achieve emotional sobriety; to get *sober,* in the fullest sense of the word, become: "*Well balanced, realistic, sensible, dignified, and rational; not driven to extremes in emotion or thought."*

If we truly understand that an addictive lifestyle has only four possible endings: *more rehabs, more suffering, jails, or death,* then our choice to become addiction survivors is made out of necessity, not virtue.

If sanity prevails, hopefully, we swallow our pride and seek guidance from people who have been able to transform their cravings for pills, alcohol, or drugs into a craving for freedom, honesty, and integrity.

What other options do we have? Just one!

We can stay on the *Relapse Roller Coaster Ride,* and continue playing Russian Roulette with our drug of choice.

THE WAY OF THE WARRIOR

The Way of the Warrior, even for us reluctant ones, is in sharp contrast to the way of our culture which is obsessed with *looking* good rather than *being* good. We're more concerned about the appearance of our "package" than its contents.

We spend billions of dollars a year on cosmetics, hair styles, wigs, toupees, plastic surgery, clothes, fragrances, and jewelry to look good, *hoping* that we will be noticed, accepted, or loved by others.

This creates a great conflict because the image we present to the *outer* world is a mask.

"More than most people, the alcoholic leads a double life. He is very much the actor. To the outer world, he presents his stage character. This is the one he likes his fellows to see." *(A.A. Page 73)*

WHAT ABOUT OUR INNER WORLD?

Behind the mask are feelings of worthlessness, not being good enough, low self-esteem, anxiety, depression, and varying degrees of self-hatred.

Along with this comes an emotional volcano that contains a mixture of rage, anger, fear, self-pity, despair, guilt, shame, and resentments. It can't be otherwise - because many of us have been victims of physical, mental, emotional, or sexual abuse, and before coming to the Fellowship, we spent years lying, cheating, and stealing time or money from those who loved and trusted us.

In addition to this, the advertising industry feeds on our fears of rejection and abandonment.

We need to use a special type of fragrance, wear a certain style *fear* of clothing, or drive a certain type of car to be accepted by others.

In our Twelve Step program, what we seek is life, *a way of life* which draws us out of our self-centered existence where what matters most can no longer be sacrificed for that which matters least.

HOW DO WE DEVELOP A WARRIOR MENTALITY?

By just not picking up a drink or drug? No
By avoiding people, places or things that act as triggers? No

Not exactly!

Anyone who offers such a simple solution is misguided, because we must first bring the mind under control, and this - is no simple task. The original members of A.A. were keenly aware that:

"*The main problem centers in the mind.*" *(A.A. P 22)*

Imagine standing in front of a gold mine.

The owner of the mine tells you that if you go inside the mine, and work very hard, you will become rich.

But there is a cost to gaining access to the mine. *You must not drink or use drugs.* To do this, it is suggested that you *avoid* all triggers.

But *avoidance* won't make you rich.

To become rich, you have to pick up a sledge hammer and chisel instead of a pill, drink, or drug, and then, you have to do the work.

To become addiction survivors, we must do the work of going *deep inside* our mind, heart, and soul and reconnect with the core values that enrich our lives. We must own them, live them, and hold ourselves accountable to them. If we do this, then, like the original members of A.A. we can reach a point in our recovery journey where we too will be able to say: "*The problem has been removed. It does not exist for us.*" *(A.A. Page 85).*

If we choose not to do this, we will never have a future, just a regrettable past that will continue to repeat itself, over and over again.

In order to climb the mountains that lead to victory over the obsessive thoughts, compulsive feelings, and physical cravings that control and dominate our lives, we must follow the path of the warrior.

We must train ourselves, day by day to be a little bit more honest, a little bit more courageous, a little bit more compassionate, a little bit more forgiving, a little bit more trusting.

Sir Edmund Hillary, the first man to climb Mount Everest, did not just stand at the bottom of the mountain, take one leap, and land on top. He spent years practicing, climbing one mountain after another to learn the skills required to reach his goal.

For us to become addiction survivors, we too must climb many mountains before we can experience the "promises" of the Twelve Steps. *(A.A. Page 83)*

In mountain climbing, climbers tie themselves to each other with ropes. If someone slips, they haul them back up to a secure place.

Within our Fellowship, if we slip into old attitudes and behaviors, someone is there to pull us up, or we are there to pull them up. Like the Marines and Navy Seals, we too are a band of brothers.

There is no greater satisfaction than being part of a Fellowship of men and women who support, help, and encourage each other to develop the core values it takes to function at the highest levels we are capable of as human beings, to soar like an eagle, to be free. *Until we discover our wings, we have no purpose in life.* Until we learn how to soar, to rise above the problems and challenges we encounter on our journey, we will never really understand what a privilege it is to be a human being, or perhaps a spiritual being, having a human experience.

BREAKING UP IS HARD TO DO

One of the things that makes us different from social drinkers is that we have a "relationship" with alcohol, as well as other drugs. At many meetings, I have heard people compare this relationship to someone who has a secret mistress or lover. But the relationship isn't the problem. *It's our attachment and dependence on this relationship that's the problem.* Whether a bird's leg is attached to a shoelace, string, or rope is insignificant, because they all keep the bird from flying. Until the attachment is broken, the bird will never fly.

Until we break our attachment to using alcohol and drugs *as an escape* from the painful realities of life, we will never be free. But it's important to understand that freedom comes with a price.

It requires a change in vision and attitude.

Many of us view ourselves as powerless, as a leaf blowing in the wind; manipulated by forces beyond our control. Often, we have no expectation of finding or experiencing anything better. The story of our lives seems to be that we are born, we are here for a period of time, and during our stay we are *victims* of powerful physical, mental, and emotional forces. Then, one day, we die. For most of us, one hundred years from now, no one will even know we existed. The quantum shift in vision and attitude that recovery offers us is this:

- Kelly -

We are not just a leaf blowing in the wind. We are the tree, filled with beauty, dignity, grace, strength, and purpose.

As we make progress in our recovery, we become more conscious and aware of the *Life Force* flowing through us. We stop being energy vampires, draining the life out of those we love, due to our addiction. In transforming the darkness of our addiction into the light of recovery our guilt and shame gets transformed into great compassion. How does this happen? Because we understand, from our own personal experience, the destructive power of cravings, resentments, fear, anger, guilt, loneliness, and despair. We understand how easy it is to rationalize lying, cheating, and stealing.

As the leaves of fear, anger, shame, guilt, resentment, and deceit begin to fall from our tree, the branches of imagination, intuition, and creativity begin to flourish. In essence, we become less self-centered. We become part of the solution instead of the problem.

In helping others get off the *Relapse Roller Coaster Ride*, we find meaning and purpose for our lives. When we help another alcoholic or addict become free from the slavery of addiction, it's like dropping a rock in a pond. It creates a ripple effect which can continue to impact future generations, long after we are gone.

Picasso has a series of paintings called *The Blues*. One of them shows a woman sitting naked, in a fetal position, with moonlight illuminating her body. The first time I saw that painting, I said: "That's me!"

I finally saw an image of someone whose body language mirrored what I was feeling: isolated, depressed, bored, and alone in the universe.

Imagine being in that room with me, listening to my tale of woe; telling you that the foul smells and unrelenting noise were driving me crazy, that I wanted to die, that I just couldn't take it one more day. Imagine telling me:

"Kelly, there's a door behind you. It's not locked. It's open, and you can leave - any time you want to."

What I would have experienced at that moment was not a sense of joy, not a sense of freedom, not a sense of gratitude, but an absolute sense of terror. Living in the darkness of addiction has many unpleasant side effects. But it has one major advantage. It's predictable. Tomorrow, will be just like today. No hits! No runs! No errors! Nothing to risk. Just another day of numbing our mind and emotions, hoping - we can make it through the night.

On October 8, 1975, I found the courage to leave that room. I felt like someone who had been physically and emotionally crippled; someone who was going to have to go through the growing pains of learning how to walk and feel all over again.

What did I find when I walked out of that room? I found you! I found someone who had experienced and survived the panic and terror I was feeling. I found someone who didn't judge or condemn me.

I found someone who wanted to know if I was ready to reach out, take their hand, and not look back. I found someone who wanted to know if I was willing to believe that, just as there isn't enough darkness in all the galaxies of the universe to put out the light of one small candle - there wasn't enough darkness in all the galaxies of my guilt and shame to put out the light of *hope* I'd find in a circle of friends standing in the light of freedom.

THE WARRIOR'S PRAYER

"Grant that I may become beautiful within, and that whatever outward things I have may be in harmony with the spirit inside me. May I understand that it is only the wise who are truly rich." (Socrates)

As water in a stream flows down a mountain, it encounters stones and rocks of different sizes. It doesn't engage in debates with them. It doesn't get angry. It doesn't yell at the rocks or curse at them. It doesn't try to smash them into tiny pieces. It simply flows by the rocks and stones because water naturally and automatically chooses the easiest and most direct way around each and every obstacle it encounters.

As we make progress in our recovery journey, our goal is to become more like the water - because we will encounter many obstacles. They will come in all shapes and sizes; some big, some small. With the Power we gain access to through the Twelve Steps, we gradually become more like the stream. No need to engage in arguments. No need make angry demands. No need to lash out. More often than not, we begin to flow past the problems we encounter. How do we do this?

We do this by going to meetings and "listening" to the messages we need to hear, or carrying a message that someone else needs to hear. We do this by meditating, which is a "maintenance" Step. Addiction is a brain disease and meditation, in addition to healing the brain, *quiets the mind, calms the emotions, and relaxes the body.* It gives us access to the Power we need to seek the natural path around each obstacle we encounter.

Many of us have used drugs, alcohol, sex, pornography, money, food, and gambling to fill the void we felt inside us. As a last resort many of us tried to fill that void with a relationship. The poem Eve points to the truth we need to learn before we begin our recovery journey.

- Radical Recovery -

EVE

I couldn't find
Self-worth or acceptance
Within
So I sought it in another
And called it
Love
Until the pain of suffocating
Dwarfed
The fear of being alone.

No pleasure palace
No lotto luck
No bedroom ecstasy
Could displace the pain
Of the wounded child
Inside me.

Innocent eyes
Studded
With cataracts of shame
Blinded me
To the light of love
Residing
In the chamber of my heart
To the sage's wisdom
Inscribed on its walls

*Recovery is a journey
Not a destination.*

MYTH 1

ADDICTION IS A BAD HABIT NOT A DISEASE

"I have learned this. It is not what one does that is wrong, but what one becomes as a consequence of it." (Oscar Wilde)

- Radical Recovery -

The cover of the book has an image of the Phoenix.

In Egyptian mythology,

the Phoenix is an immortal bird.

When it dies,

it bursts into flames,

and is reborn from its own ashes.

To Rise From the Ashes of the Phoenix

means

To make a miraculous comeback.

If you believe that you are ready

To Rise From the Ashes of Addiction,

and

make a miraculous comeback

then

Welcome to Radical Recovery.

T**HE WORD "RADICAL" CAN BRING** to mind images of extreme anarchy or violent revolution, but according to Webster's Dictionary, the word radical has a much softer connotation. It is defined as:
   1. Getting to the **root** or **origin** of something.
   2. Thoroughgoing, as regards a change from accepted or traditional forms.

When chemotherapy was first introduced as a method of treating cancer, it was considered a very *radical* way of getting to the root of the disease, because the "chemo" part of the therapy is a poison. But the poison works. It kills cancer cells. Unfortunately, it also kills healthy cells which results in very unpleasant side effects. The person infected with the poison most often experiences hair loss, nausea, vomiting, etc.

The good news here is that, in many cases, the temporary pain and discomfort that comes with the treatment puts the disease into full remission. The odds of staying in full remission increase, if the cancer survivor does certain other things such as eating healthy foods, exercising, taking prescribed medications, vitamin supplements, and of course, no smoking.

The bad news for us alcoholics and drug addicts is that the odds of becoming a cancer survivor are much greater than the odds of becoming an addiction survivor. Why?

Well, just as we don't consider cigarette smoking a "disease," on some level we tend to link cigarette smoking with alcohol and drugs. Bad habits we would like to get rid of - some day in the future.

Addiction is not just a disease. Left untreated, it is a *terminal* disease. But we really don't believe this, even though millions of addicts and alcoholics have proven this to us over and over again. Some of the more prominent ones include: Marilyn Monroe, Elvis Presley, Anna Nicole Smith, Janis Joplin, Jimmy Hendricks, John Belushi, etc. While we may give lip service to the idea that we have a terminal disease, our actions and attitudes tell a different story. For example, at meetings newcomers are often told, "Don't rush into the Steps."

Once, while attending a meeting on Step 4: *"Made A Fearless and Searching Moral Inventory of Ourselves,"* a man who had not had a drink in eight years, said, "It took me more than five years to complete Step 4. You didn't get sick overnight; you're not going to get well over night. Easy does it."

Bad advice! He may not have had a drink in eight years, but he sure didn't have anything I wanted.

Imagine being diagnosed with cancer, and going to your first meeting of *Cancer Survivors Anonymous.* You let everyone know that you are a newcomer. Can you imagine anyone in that room telling you, "Don't rush into getting treatment. Your cancer didn't happen overnight. It's not going to disappear overnight. So, easy does it."

If we really believed that we had a terminal disease, we would read the book, *How To Become An Addiction Survivor,* otherwise known as *Alcoholics Anonymous.* We would approach treatment with the same desire, motivation, and passion that someone diagnosed with cancer seeks treatment, the same desire, motivation, and passion that someone who is drowning reaches for a life preserver. But we don't. Why not? The answer should obvious - brain damage. Another reason why we have Step 2, *"Came to believe that a Power greater than ourselves could restore us to sanity."*

As the chemicals in alcohol and drugs kill more and more of our brain cells, our *primitive brain* takes over. The primitive brain works on the philosophy of, "If it feels good - do it."

Just as an infant has no access to speech, we have no access to the memory of what happened the last time we picked up a pill, drink, or drug. Here's what happens as the disease progresses.

We go into a coma, which is defined as: "A state of prolonged unconsciousness, including a lack of response to stimuli, from which it is impossible to rouse a person." This is pretty accurate because:

We look - but we don't see.
We hear - but we don't listen.
We touch - but we don't feel.

Another reason we fail to believe we have a terminal disease is that - we don't believe that rules and odds apply to us. *We like to make up our own rules and odds and about life.* For example, in addition to not really believing that addiction, left untreated, is a terminal disease, we really don't believe that cigarette smoking causes lung cancer, emphysema, heart disease, etc. If we did, we would stop smoking, but about 90 percent of the people who seek treatment for alcohol or drugs are also addicted to nicotine. I sympathize! I smoked two packs a day for many years.

The *Disease of Chemical Dependency,* whether it's an addiction to pills, alcohol, drugs, nicotine, or the comfort we get from eating unhealthy foods, is *cunning, baffling, and powerful.* That's one reason why the relapse rate is so high.

But, was it always this way?

Let's look at the history of our fellowship. The original members of A.A. tell us:

"Of alcoholics who came to A.A. and really tried, 50% got sober at once, and remained that way; 25% sobered up after some relapses, and among the remainder, those who stayed on with A.A. showed improvement." *(A.A. Page xx)*

According to the U.S. *Substance Abuse and Mental Health Services Administration,* 80% of the drug addicts and alcoholics coming out of treatment centers relapse within twelve months; some, the first day, (www.ncadi.samhsa.gov). HBO's documentary, REHAB, states that the relapse rate is much worse, more than 90%. Either way, the cost to the U.S economy, including actual treatment, time lost from work, wrecked cars, imprisonment, etc. is about $180 billion a year.

The reason we need such a "radical" approach to recovery is that we need a change from *accepted and traditional forms.*

While an 80% to 90% failure rate may be very traditional, I believe it is unacceptable; that's why I am writing this book; that's why I have pioneered new, cutting edge approaches to treating addiction.

The problem we face is much bigger than pills, alcohol, or drugs. These substances are just *symptoms* of the problem, and so long as we continue to treat the *symptom*, we will continue to relapse, and we will continue to die from this disease. The following story illustrates the point.

A man who grew up in a small rural community visited a large city for the first time. When he returned, his friends asked him: "What was it like?"

He responded:

"Such tall buildings - such small people."

If you were asked to write a report on our society's achievements, you could state that:

1. We have found cures for many diseases.
2. We have put men on the moon.
3. We have made great scientific discoveries, and
4. We have made many significant technological advancements:

- E-mail and texting give us instant communication.
- Microwave ovens have freed up hours of time spent on food preparation.
- With high-tech cell phones we can call anyone, anytime, anywhere.
- The internet gives us instant access to information on any subject.
- Wall Street Warriors created billions of dollars to help people buy homes.

BUT OUR "PROGRESS" HAS COME WITH A PRICE

The Wall Street Warriors, driven by greed, created a mortgage crisis that sent millions of Americans into bankruptcy, and left many of us with homes that are worth far less than what we paid for them.

With the internet, sexual predators have gained access to our children.

With online gambling, porno sites, and chat rooms, we can feed our addictive appetites twenty-four hours a day.

Combining texting and driving has proved to be a lethal combination.

With microwave ovens we eat more, but we communicate less.

Obesity has become the number one cause of preventable death in the United States.

With all the advances we have made, not too many great men and women have emerged. Those few that have demonstrated greatness, through service to mankind, seldom made the headlines.

Many of our "heroes" have fallen: Tiger Woods, Bernie Madoff, Rupert Murdoch, and platoons of senators, governors, mayors, congressmen, clergy, lawyers, doctors, high school teachers, community leaders, and army generals who got caught with their hands is someone's pants or someone's pocket.

How does this happen? We don't just go running away from our core values. We drift away, a day at a time, and one day we wake up in the middle of a nightmare, in a place we never meant to be.

The springboard for getting back to the core values that brought us joy, peace, self-esteem, and a healthy form of self-love almost always comes in the form of a *crisis*. We hit a mental, emotional, physical, financial, or spiritual bottom.

The Chinese use a combination of two characters for the word crisis. These two characters designate *danger* and *opportunity*. This seems to be true of every crisis. For some of us, the crisis is like a speed bump, for others it's a brick wall. But either way, it is a turning point. Depending on how well we make the turn, we can find danger, opportunity, or death. We need to *re-mind* ourselves, and be *re-minded* about:

1. Our purpose - Conform our will to God's will.
2. Our goal - Victory over alcohol and drugs x find God
3. The solution - To grow along spiritual lines.

This is why it is important to seek out Step and Big Book meetings where the focus is on the solution, and avoid BGT meetings, *Bad Group Therapy*, where the focus is on: "Who has a problem they would like to discuss?" With therapy, a person is seeking a *solution* for their problem. With meetings, many times, the person speaking is not seeking a solution. They just want to dump their story on the group. We can dump our stories on sponsors, friends, clergy, and psychologists. They are usually good listeners. This is the right place to do our dumping. According to Bill Wilson:

"Sobriety - freedom from alcohol, through the teaching and practice of A.A.'s Twelve Steps, is the sole purpose of the group. If we don't stick to this cardinal principle, we shall almost certainly collapse. And if we collapse, we can't help anyone." *(As Bill Sees It - Page 79)*

Was Bill misguided here?

Aren't meetings where we go to share all our *personal problems* with the group? NO

When newcomers get triggered at meetings by graphic alcohol and drug stories, when they get depressed by all the negativity, when the relapse rate is a national disgrace, we have to wonder:

Was Bill right about the sole purpose of the group?

Have we forgotten this *cardinal principle*?

Have we again taken the easier softer way?

Have we collapsed?

One of the greatest assets we possess as human beings is our ability to adapt.

If our homes are destroyed by tornadoes, fires, earthquakes, or hurricanes, we adapt to temporary surroundings.

What initially feels very awkward and strange, gradually becomes a permanent part of our daily routine.

Over time, we stop comparing our old way of living with our new way of living.

A new reality emerges.

That's what happened to me!

As my alcohol and drug use increased, and I became more and more mentally impaired, the door to that old way of living began to close - slowly.

I didn't see it coming.

As long as I could see *any* opening in the door, I was able to con myself into believing that I didn't have a problem. But the day eventually arrived when the millions of brain cells I killed, finally took their toll.

I began to feel like the popcorn machine Andrew Auw describes in his poem, *Out Of Order*.

Here, he comes upon the scene of a young mother trying to explain to her four year old boy that the popcorn machine is broken; that it just isn't capable of giving out its contents.

I believe this poem mirrors the *crisis* we face as alcoholics and drug addicts.

- Kelly -

OUT OF ORDER

"You can't get any popcorn, child.
The machine is out of order.
See, there's a sign on the machine."

But he didn't understand.
After all,
He had the desire.
He had the money.
He could see the popcorn inside the machine.
And yet somehow, somewhere,
Something was wrong
Because
He couldn't get the popcorn.
The boy walked back with his mother,
And he wanted to cry.
I too felt like weeping,
Weeping for people who have become
Locked in, jammed, and broken
Filled with goodness
That other people need and want
And yet may never come to enjoy
Because
Something has gone wrong
Inside.

MYTH 2

I AM DIFFERENT FROM YOU

"These are the only genuine ideas, the ideas of the shipwrecked. All the rest is rhetoric, posturing, farce." (Jose Ortega y Gasset)

- *Kelly* -

Wˢᴱ ᴀʀᴇ ᴅɪғғᴇʀᴇɴᴛ, ʙᴜᴛ ᴛʜᴇ same, in that each of us is born with a spark of the divine inside us. Our efforts should be directed toward fanning this spark until it becomes a flame, and then a torch, that converts the darkness of addiction into the light of freedom.

Meditation ignites the spark of the Divine inside us.

If we are willing to make it part of our daily routine, like brushing our teeth, it becomes a flame, and then a torch, that enables us to live balanced lives.

Recovery is about replacing old self-destructive habits, with new positive habits that enable, empower, inspire, and motivate us to live happy, useful, and productive lives.

How much time did you spend each day thinking about, obtaining, using, or recovering from the excesses of alcohol or drugs? If you were to now use that time to meditate, you would probably be meditating for many hours every day. So, "I don't have time to mediate," is not an acceptable excuse.

Meditation takes us on a journey of *self*-discovery.

This is why it's a *Maintenance Step*, something we should do every day because it opens the door to a world of imagination, intuition, creativity, and power. It gives us access to a Force and Strength that is *much more powerful* than our addiction, *much more powerful* than the obsessive thoughts, compulsive feelings, and physical cravings that control and dominate our lives.

Just as healthy foods give our body the energy and power it needs to perform at the highest level, meditation gives us access to the energy and power we need, as human beings, to perform at the highest level.

It keeps our body, mind, senses, and emotions in balance.

In going through the *dis-covery* process that meditation provides, we become enlightened.

We discover that *we are not our body*; that our body is the *house* in which we live. Body is the temple

LIFE AS A HOUSE

Think of a house as a metaphor for recovery. There may be aspects of your house that you find lacking. Perhaps the roof leaks, there are holes in some of the walls, the plumbing doesn't work, or the electrical outlets are without power.

These problems are like the character defects that make our lives unmanageable.

When we stop drinking and using drugs, it's like painting the outside of the house, and putting a sign on front lawn which says: NEW AND IMPROVED - but the underling reality remains the same.

If the inside of the house is in shambles, then no sign in the world will make a bit of difference. The only thing that will really improve the situation is to make the necessary repairs.

The Twelve Steps are the home improvement tools we need to make repairs in the house of our life. Just as we can create comfortable homes by replacing worn out plumbing, patching damaged walls, and making electrical repairs, we can recreate our lives.

As we continue this process of *self-discovery*, we become less concerned about what people think about the *outside* of our house and more concerned about what's *inside*.

In the early years of recovery, as we continue to practice the spiritual principles of the Twelve Steps, as a way of life, our brain begins to heal from the terrific beating and battering it received by the chemicals in pills, alcohol, and drugs.

We begin to wake up.

We start to become *conscious* and *aware* of the core values we stored far way in the basement of our house.

With meditation, we discover that "spiritual principles, plus the program of action will solve all our problems."(A.A. Page 42)

To put this in perspective, use your imagination.

Picture a chariot, a charioteer, and five horses.

THE CHARIOT is your body.

THE FIVE HORSES are your five senses.

THE CHARIOTEER human intelligence, is your mind.

THE REINS are your *Spirit*, a "higher" form of Intelligence.

As you can see, we have much in common.

Our bodies desire pleasure and comfort.

Our senses take delight in providing our bodies with all the pleasure and comfort it wants: food, sex, alcohol, drugs, etc.

At the beginning, it's a very enjoyable experience, but over time, as we let our senses, the horses, run our lives, we lose balance and control.

We get lost.

We end up in a great deal of pain.

We cry out for help.

The *Charioteer*, hearing our cry for help, picks up the reins. The *rational* part of our mind takes control. All goes well for a while, but the rational part of our mind has a significant limitation.

When the senses pull on it, it can justify and rationalize that it's okay to loosen its grip on the reins and permit a *little* self indulgence. And a *little* self-indulgence is good.

But when it comes to pills, alcohol, sex, and drugs, as a species, we don't indulge, we devour, we over indulge.

For example, obesity and nicotine addiction are two top causes of preventable death in the U.S.

THE REINS, our Spirit, can be weak or strong. Step 11 states:

"We sought through prayer and meditation to improve our conscious contact with God *as we understood Him,* praying only for knowledge of His will for us and the power to carry that out."

Step 11 is a Maintenance Step. This means, we should do it every day. It provides us with the two resources we need to keep our torch burning, to keep our lives in balance, prayer *and* meditation.

This is the exercise, the *workout* we need to do each day to make our *Spirit* strong, to develop our spiritual muscle.

The horses, our senses, will, by nature, want to go down many self-indulgent paths that provide us with instant gratification.

If you have been *working out*, your *Spirit* has the strength and power to redirect your senses down paths where you are able to maintain your core values.

When you cry out for help, and the rational part of your mind says, "Pull back on the reins," your *Spirit*, which is your *Higher Self*, has the power to resist, to keep your life in balance, not over indulging, not under indulging, balanced.

If you haven't been working out, you will go back down that same self-indulgent path.

When the fun is over, and you are *again* filled with remorse, guilt, and shame, you will cry out for help. But the day may come when even this is no longer an option.

Instead, you may choose to wallow in self-pity and continue to numb the feelings of remorse, guilt, and shame with more pills, alcohol, or drugs.

How much *spiritual muscle* will you develop if you *don't* perform the exercises in this Maintenance Step? None!

When we attend our first A.A. or N.A. meeting, many of us tend to notice the differences rather than the similarities between ourselves and the other people present at the meeting.

For many of us the "differences" are the YETS.

I haven't had a DUI - yet.
I haven't lost custody of my children - yet.
I haven't been to jail - yet.
I haven't lost my self-respect - yet.
I haven't lost friends due to my addiction - yet.
I haven't thought about suicide - yet.
I haven't stolen money to feed my addiction - yet.
I haven't lost my driver's license - yet.
I haven't traded sex for drugs - yet.
I haven't lost a job due to my addiction - yet.
I haven't lost a marriage due to my addiction - yet.
I haven't damaged my body as a result of my addiction - yet.
Let's see if you can relate to what you will find in:

A CIRCLE OF FRIENDS

I don't care how much money you make, or what kind of car you drive.

I want to know how many times you've gone to bed at night and prayed - that you wouldn't wake up in the morning.

I want to know if your well of compassion is deep enough to forgive yourself and others, for being human.

I want to know if you have the courage to stand in a circle of friends who have transformed the comfortable and familiar slavery of addiction into a burning desire for honesty, integrity, peace, humility, and freedom.

- Kelly -

I don't care about the highs you got from shooting heroin, popping pills, snorting cocaine, or drinking alcohol.

I want to know about the lows you felt the morning after, when you looked in the mirror and *remembered* what you said or did the night before; the panic you felt if you ever woke up not knowing where you were, how you got there, or the person sleeping next to you.

I want to know if you've learned the lesson that there is no future in addiction, just a regrettable past that keeps repeating itself, over and over again; that when you numb your ability to feel pain, you also numb your ability to feel joy.

I want to know if you understand that there isn't enough Scotch in Scotland, Cocaine in Columbia, or Opium in Afghanistan to fill the hole inside you; that inner peace comes from *taming*, not *feeding*, your cravings, compulsions, and obsessions.

I don't care if you're a Leo, Aquarius, or Libra.

I want to know if you're willing to embrace and comfort the shell-shocked child inside you, the child who lost its innocence when a sacred trust was violated.

I want to know if you are willing to reclaim the courage of that two-year-old who learned how to walk without using a crutch; who, after falling down, got right back up again.

I want to know if you can still access the laughter and spontaneity of that kid, who, without being self-conscious, or worrying what others would think, would race along ocean shores and play tag with waves as they crashed along the beach.

I don't care if you're afraid of being hurt, who isn't?

I want to know how you conned yourself into believing that emotional and spiritual starvation is less painful than the risk of loving, or being loved.

I want to know if you are willing to grow beyond that false sense of security you feel when you numb your feelings, and isolate yourself behind the walls of your safe and solitary prison.

I don't care if you're infected with the disease to please and be accepted by everyone you meet.

I want to know if you can please and accept yourself, let go of the lie that you're not worthy of unconditional love; stop being seduced, battered, and betrayed by a counterfeit lover who

unleashes tidal waves of insatiable cravings which kill trust, abort hope, shatter dreams, and transform a few minutes of heavenly bliss into weeks, months, or years of a hellish nightmare.
I don't care if you never received the love you needed.
    I want to know if you're willing to stop playing the role of victim, and give yourself the love you never got; if you understand that behind each mask of manicured manners and proper pretense is a person - just like you: someone with a story, someone whose heart has been broken, someone whose smiling eyes camouflage a lake of unshed tears, someone who has sought out imaginary lovers to comfort them with illusions of intimacy and satisfy unspoken passions and desires, someone who carries the weight of guilt, shame, regret, and sorrow.
    I want to know if you can stop whipping yourself for failing to measure up to illusions of perfection.
I don't care how many notches you have on your detox belt.
    I want to know if you understand that you are not your disease, but simply a person with a disease, that you are not *powerless* over your disease, that you are power-full; that the same Power which transforms an ugly caterpillar into a beautiful butterfly, can transform your cravings for pills, alcohol, or drugs into a craving for courage, to do what it takes, to become an addiction survivor.
    I want to know if you are willing to awaken and nurture the *Sleeping Giant* deep inside you by sitting still for twenty minutes a day, until you truly love the person you become in that time of sacred solitude.
I don't care about the terror you feel when you have to face a day without the possibility of being numb.
    I want to know if you're ready to reach out, take my hand, and not look back; if you can believe that, just as there isn't enough darkness in all the galaxies of the universe to put out the light of one small candle, there isn't enough darkness in all the galaxies of your guilt and shame to put out the light of *hope* you'll find in a circle of friends standing in the light of freedom.
    In addition to being able to relate to some of the thoughts and feelings expressed here, there are:

Some Other Things We May Have In Common

As a group, here's how the original members of A.A. described themselves:

"Almost without exception, alcoholics are tortured by loneliness. Even before our drinking got bad and people began to cut us off, nearly all of us suffered from the feeling that we didn't quite belong." *(Twelve Steps and Twelve Traditions Page 57)*

On a personal level, I always had this feeling deep down in my gut, scared. I was afraid:

That I wouldn't be accepted.
That I didn't quite measure up to my friends.
That I was always on the outside looking in.
That I was never a part of what was going on.
All these feelings vanished the day I had my first drink.
The *magic* happened!
New and beautiful feelings exploded inside me, like fireworks on the Fourth of July.
Prior to that moment, I had always felt like a jig saw puzzle, with one piece missing.
That night, the missing piece fell into place.
I was okay.
I was able to talk, laugh, dance, and enjoy being in my own skin.
That feeling of inferiority, which had always been with me, just vanished, like the beautiful woman behind the magician's cape.
For the first time in my life, I didn't feel scared.
I felt alive... inside.
All the barriers were removed.
I fit in.
I was drawn to people, and they were drawn to me.
It has been said that, it's never too late to have a happy childhood.
How do we do that?
Perhaps the answer can be found in the poem, *Lost and Found*.

LOST AND FOUND

The father [God] proudly lifted his little girl [Me] for all the world to see.
He marveled at her innocence, he loved her, unconditionally.
But demands were made as she grew older.
She had to conform; he began to mold her.
The forms were soon made in which she would fit.
She learned when to stand, she learned when to sit.
She soon lost her spirit, she soon found her place.
She joined the great herd; she learned to keep pace.
The unconditional love which was given at birth
Was replaced by the strings that determined her worth.
But soon, the strings, which held her so tight
Began to break, and she began to fight.

She fought her way back to the child that she lost.
Now, she's reaping the rewards of paying the cost.

She's become a new person, she's found her direction.
She's no longer striving for total perfection.
She's looking at life through a new pair of glasses.
She's learned to accept each day as it passes.
And here is the message she shares with us all:

To learn how to walk, you must stumble and fall.

With pain comes growth

MYTH 3

WE ARE POWERLESS OVER OUR ADDICTION

"When nothing seems to help, I go look at a stonecutter hammering away at his rock; perhaps a hundred times without as much as a crack showing in it. Yet at the hundred and first blow it will split in two, and I know it was not that blow that did it - but all the blows that had gone before." (Jacob Riis)

IF WE ARE *POWERLESS* OVER our addiction, then:
- Let's tell the insurance companies to stop paying $40 billion a year for treatment because treatment doesn't work for people who believe they are *powerless* over their addiction.
- Let's shut down all the treatment centers in the country, because they have nothing to offer the weak and *powerless* alcoholics and addicts who come to them.
- Lets close the doors of N.A. and A.A., and the more than 150 other Twelve Step Programs because, if we are *powerless*, why even try?
- Let's tell those who suffer from addictions to go home, and just wait for the end to come, because there is absolutely nothing they can do to help themselves **recover** from their addiction. They are victims of a terminal disease that will kill them. But we need to let them know that before it kills them, it will put them, and those they love, through a great deal more pain and suffering.

If this were true, I would rather drink until my liver rotted, or hope and pray that I overdosed the next time I used drugs.

Does this mean we can learn how to "control" our drinking or drug use? Not exactly!

It is important to understand:
1. What we *are* powerless over.
2. What we are *not* powerless over; and
3. What the difference is between *powerlessness* and *control*.

But before doing this, it's important to understand the *dilemma* we face as alcoholics and drug addicts: "Lack of power - that was our dilemma." *(A.A. P 45)*

If I am powerless over something, there is nothing I can do about it. On the other hand, if I simply *lack power*, there is something I can do. I can take the necessary *steps* to gain access to the power I need.

POWERLESSNESS VS. CONTROL

There was a time in my life when I could drink a six pack of beer with some friends, go home, and not need to drink another six pack before I went to bed. I had power.

As my tolerance increased, I needed *more* to get the same effect. I began to have *less* power.

As I consumed more and more alcohol, I finally reached the point where I became *powerless,* because once I had that first drink, I continued to drink until either I was gone, or the booze was gone.

I became "powerless" over what happened next. Why? Well, after the first drink, the cravings kicked in. Then, the only thing that mattered in my life was getting another drink.

I was at a meeting once where someone said:

"I am powerless over whether or not the sun will rise or set."

I thought, "That's insane. The rising and setting of the sun isn't a *powerless i*ssue, it's a control issue." **I never had the power** to determine whether or not the sun was going to rise or set, so how could I have *less* power?

I thought about all the other things I never had the power to control, the weather, economy, wars, people, so again, how could I have *less* power?

WHAT IS IT THAT WE ARE "POWERLESS" OVER?

When we admit that we are "powerless" over pills, alcohol, or drugs, what is it that we are really admitting?

We are admitting that:
1. We have a problem.
2. We have tried to solve the problem using the **human resources** available to us.
3. We have been unsuccessful in the many attempts we made to solve our problem.

What **human resources** do we have access to that can help us solve our problem, our addiction to pills, drugs, or alcohol? There are three of them, and they are all very, very powerful:
1. MIND
2. EMOTIONS
3. SPIRIT

THE MIND

If we just had a brain, like many of the animals that roam the planet, we would still be living in caves, living by instinct alone.
Our mind functions at a higher level:
1. We are the only species on the planet that can *think* about what we are going to do two weeks from now, or what we did two weeks ago.
2. As a result of having a mind we can imagine, plan, and create *Two Twin Towers* in New York City, but we can also imagine, plan, and create a way to take down those *Two Twin Towers*.

    The mind is like a battery. It has positive and negative energy. The negative, or dark side of our mind, is our ability as human beings to *rationalize* lying, cheating, stealing, raping, being unfaithful, driving drunk or high, or going into a movie theatre at midnight and killing or wounding scores of innocent people.

On the positive side, we have invented all the technology of the last two hundred years: air conditioning, electricity, indoor plumbing, flight, microwaves, cell phones, automobiles, the internet, etc. We have put men on the moon, successfully performed heart transplants, and found cures for diseases.

Why, having such a *powerful* resource as the **mind**, can't it help us solve our problem with addiction?

Think about all the times you used the **power of your mind**, your ability to *reason* and said, "I am done with drinking or using drugs, it's creating problems for me."

Did the **power of your mind**, your ability to *reason* help you solve your problem? Obviously, the answer is "No!" But why not?

Because addiction is a **brain disease**, and our brain gets *hijacked* by the **chemicals** in pills, alcohol, and drugs.

It has been said that Chicago has two seasons, winter and road repair. The damage done to our brain by the **chemicals** in pills, alcohol and drugs is similar to the damage done to Chicago's streets and highways every winter. By the time spring arrives, there are a lot of pot holes that have to be filled.

By the time we are humble enough to ask for help with our addiction, the **chemicals** in pills, alcohol, and drugs have created lots of *pot holes* in our brain, and our brain is in desperate need of road repair.

With this severely damaged and impaired brain, we then attend our first meeting. But unlike the original members of A.A., we are usually not offered the **hope** that *we can recover* from "a seemingly hopeless state of mind and body," and live as free men and women.

Instead, it's more like being sentenced to spend the rest of lives walking around with a ball and chain attached to our leg because most often we are told:

"You will never recover."

"It will be a daily battle for the rest of your life."

"Your best (not your worst) thinking got you here."

This is in sharp contrast the *Recovery Power Mindset* used by the original members of A.A. where the goal was *victory* over alcohol.

How does one *find* a spiritual experience? One seeks! After being sentenced to walk around with a ball and chain attached to their legs, any newcomer who has an issue with *God* is usually told that they can turn to *a power less than themselves* to get restored to sanity, inanimate objects like chairs, pencils, or doorknobs.

Common sense would dictate that we tell newcomers who have an issue with *God*, to use the group as a higher power. Why? Because the group actually has power, the *power* of the code:

"Love and tolerance is our code." *(A.A. Page 84)*

Presented with this very negative and limiting view of recovery, and the insane idea that chairs, doorknobs, and pencils can restore them to sanity, many newcomers never come back to our Fellowship because they wonder:

"Who is more insane, me or them, and if this is 'sobriety,' do I really want what they have?"

Addiction can be defined as, "The *inability* of a person to reason effectively with himself, and implement a decision for his own well being."

As newcomers, we may have the *willingness* to recover, but we are not playing with a full deck. With an impaired brain, we don't have access to our *best* thinking due to our inability to reason effectively with ourselves. We need guidance and direction.

This is why it is so important to **read the book**, Alcoholics Anonymous where we find all the hope, motivation, and inspiration we need to achieve **victory** over our addiction to alcohol or drugs.

EMOTIONS

It's been said that love is the most powerful force in the universe.

Do you love your parents, siblings, spouse, partner, or children?

Yes?

Then shouldn't the **power of your emotion**, your love, be strong enough to stop you from drinking or using drugs?

This is a logical assumption on the part of many people, but there is a force that is *much more powerful* than logic or love, and that force is **cravings**.

When the cravings kick in, logic and love get swallowed up by the pot holes in our brain.

SPIRIT

In the movie *Cinderella Man*, Russell Crowe played the role of James Braddock, a professional fighter in the 1920's.

After becoming heavyweight champion of the world, a reporter interviewing him asked him this question,

"What motivated you to accomplish this goal?"

He responded, "Milk!"

Then there was a flashback.

We see him sitting around the kitchen table with his wife and children. It was winter, and the country had just entered the great depression of the 1930's.

No milk!

No cereal!

No heat!

No money!

These images, when he was up against the ropes being pounded by his opponent, triggered something inside him, a *burning desire* that gave him access to an exceptional source of power and strength, the **human spirit**. This *power* enabled him to overcome the obstacle standing in front of him.

In the book Alcoholics Anonymous there's a story about a man who had a *burning desire* to succeed in business.

The *desire* was so strong that it enabled him to stop drinking for 20 years.

He became very successful, retired, started to drink again, and drank himself to death in four years.

Has the **power of the human spirit** enabled you to stop drinking or using drugs?

If you are a real alcoholic or drug addict, the answer is again, "No!" So, let's review the three ways you have tried to solve your *problem* with pills, alcohol, or drugs.

1. Accessing the **power of your mind,** your ability to reason. *Strike one.*
2. Accessing the **power of your emotions**, the *love* you have for your spouse, family, or children. *Strike two.*
3. Accessing the **power of your spirit**, an *exceptional* force of power and strength. *Strike three.*

If you are like me, and the original members of A.A., you struck out trying to rely on the **human resources** available to you.

When we have tried and failed, time after time, and finally accept the fact that our human resources aren't powerful enough to help us stop drinking or using drugs, we then become humble enough to *admit* four things:

ONE

We *admit* that once put the **chemicals** in pills, alcohol, or drugs inside our bodies, we have an *allergic* reaction.

They release a tidal wave of cravings.

The **chemicals** then write the next chapter in the story of our lives. We've learned that this is a battle we can't win. Why? *Because, it's not a fair fight.*

When alcohol and drugs trigger *a chemical* reaction in our brain, cravings then take control of our lives. We lose all access to rational thought, the loving feelings we have for our spouse, partner, or families, as well as our spiritual beliefs and moral values.

TWO

We *admit* that we can't effectively manage our lives because *we have lost control* of our minds, our body, and our emotions.

The mental obsession, along with the physical cravings and compulsive feelings have become the driving forces in our lives.

The *love affair* we have with pills, alcohol, or drugs turns into an abusive relationship.

It goes something like this:

We begin to abuse the pills, alcohol, or drugs; then they begin to abuse us.

We steal time, and sometimes money, from those who love us.

We do "whatever it takes" to have a few moments of bliss together.

We cut ourselves off from the outside world and **escape** into another world, by numbing the mental, emotional, spiritual, or physical pain we are experiencing.

THREE

We *admit* that we have to find a power **greater** than the *human resources* available to us, our mind, emotions, and spirit because they completely failed us.

FOUR

We *admit* that we have *The Disease of Chemical Dependency* which, like cancer, is a terminal disease, when it is left untreated.

But we need to be aware that, before it kills us, it will continue to inflict a great deal of pain and suffering on our lives, and those we love.

Now that you understand what you are powerless over, the **chemicals** in pills, alcohol, and drugs, let's look at:

WHAT YOU ARE NOT POWERLESS OVER

1. You are not powerless over the way you THINK
2. You are not powerless over the way you FEEL, and
3. You are not powerless over the way you ACT

Does this mean that we can actually *recover* from our addiction to pills, alcohol, or drugs and live as free men and women? Absolutely!

That's what the Twelve Steps are about, a path that guides us from the slavery of addition to the freedom of recovery.

We can **recover** mentally.
We can **recover** emotionally.
We can **recover** financially.
We can **recover** relationships.
We can **recover** our integrity.
We can **recover** our self-esteem.
We can **recover** the respect of others.
We can **recover** spiritually, and in most cases,
We can **recover** physically.

There is only one thing we will never be able to recover as alcoholics and drug addicts, and that is *control*, the ability to *safely* use pills, alcohol or drugs.

At this point, you have identified:

1. What you *are* powerless over.
2. What you are *not* powerless over, and that
3. You can *recover* from your addiction to pills, alcohol or drugs.

Remember what the odds were of becoming an addiction survivor in 1935, when A.A. was founded?

"Among physicians, the general opinion seems to be that most chronic alcoholics are doomed." (A.A. Page xxx)

How did the original members overcome such tremendous odds? What approach did they use to solve the problem?

Perhaps the answer to this question can best be found in the chapter, *More About Alcoholism*, in the book *Alcoholics Anonymous*.

Dr. William Silkworth was the doctor who treated Bill Wilson and many thousands of other alcoholics and drug addicts between 1920 and 1950.

"Though not a religious person, I have profound respect for the spiritual approach in such cases as yours. For most cases, there is virtually no other solution." (A.A. Page 43)

In her book, A Return To Love, Marianne Williamson identifies what may be the greatest obstacle we face in becoming addiction survivors, our unwillingness to believe that we are power-full, just like a caterpillar. But if we want to awaken the beauty and power we have inside us, like the caterpillar, we must immerse ourselves in a cocoon. For us, the cocoon is the spiritual principles in the Twelve Steps.

It is there that we discover that:
- We are not powerless over our addiction.
- We have access to a Spiritual Force and Power inside us that is *much more powerful* than our addiction, *much more powerful* than the obsessive thoughts, compulsive feelings, and physical cravings that control and dominate our lives.

THE SPIRITUAL PRINCIPLES IN THE 12 STEPS

Imagine asking God, "What must I do to recover from my addiction to pills, alcohol, or drugs?"

Imagine getting this response, "If you want to recover what you have lost, a quiet mind and tranquil emotions, if you want to lose your fear of today, tomorrow, and the hereafter, if you want to become free from the slavery of addiction, then as each day dawns, immerse yourself in the cocoon of silence where my infinite grace, mercy, and patience will transform you as you surrender:

Your Fears
That I may fill you with
The Spirit of Courage
Your Despair
That I may fill you with
The Spirit of Hope
Your Doubts
That I may fill you with
The Spirit of Trust
Your Guilt and Shame
That I may fill you with

The Spirit of Compassion
Your Resentments
That I may fill you with
The Spirit of Forgiveness
Your Lust
That I may fill you with
The Spirit of Intimacy
Your Arrogance
That I may fill you with
The Spirit of Humility
Your Lies and Rationalizations
That I may fill you with
The Spirit of Integrity
Your Anger and Rage
That I may fill you with
The Spirit of Peace
Your Self-Pity
That I may fill you with
The Spirit of Gratitude
Your Barren Loneliness
That I may fill you with
The Spirit of Solitude
Your Self-Hatred
That I may fill you with
The Spirit of Unconditional Love.

Marianne Williamson

"Our deepest fear is not that we are inadequate.
Our deepest fear is that we are powerful beyond measure.
It is our *light*, not our *darkness* that most frightens us.
We ask ourselves: "Who am I to be brilliant, gorgeous, talented, fabulous?
Actually, who are you *not* to be?
You are a child of God.
Your playing small does not serve the world.
There is nothing enlightened about shrinking so that other people won't feel insecure around you.
We are all meant to shine, as children do.

We were born to make manifest the glory of God within us.
It's not just in some of us.
It's in everyone.
As we let our own light shine, we unconsciously give other people permission to do the same.
As we are liberated from our own fears, our presence automatically liberates others."

MYTH 4

WE NEED A HIGHER POWER TO RECOVER

"Some people want to see God with their eyes as they see a cow, and to love Him as they love their cow - for the milk, cheese, and profit it brings them. This is how it is for people who love God for the sake of outward wealth or inward comfort." (Meister Eckhart)

Do we need a Higher Power to recover? Obviously, this is not true. We don't need a power *greater* than ourselves to stop drinking our using drugs. We don't need a power greater than ourselves to have the obsessive thoughts, compulsive feelings, and physical cravings removed. Walk into almost any A.A. or N.A. meeting in the U.S. and you will hear newcomers being told that they can use a power **less than themselves** to recover their sanity.

What if... we asked newcomers if they would like to reconnect to a *Higher Self*, a *Self* they lost contact with, a *Self* that is more powerful than their addiction, a *Self* that is more forgiving, honest, and compassionate? Only a fool would object to this.

One of the biggest problems many of us face when first introduced to the *spiritual solution* presented to us in the Twelve Steps is that when we hear the word God, we think the Twelve Steps are about religion. They are not. The Twelve Steps are simply twelve spiritual principles.

This misconception, can be a major obstacle to becoming an addiction survivor.

Here are three simple metaphors that will hopefully offer you a fresh and meaningful perspective on the difference between spirituality and religion.

THE HOLE IN THE CENTER OF THE WHEEL

The hole in the center of a wheel is what makes the wheel useful.

The wheel has many spokes joining together in the central hub, but none of the spokes are as important as the **emptiness** in the middle.

The spokes represent the many different religions.

The hole in the center represents, spirituality, spiritual principles.

One has to do with form, structure, content, and beliefs.

The other is based on an *experience* which results in a "knowing" rather than a believing.

THE BANANA

Another metaphor which can be used to explain the difference between spirituality and religion is a banana.

Imagine peeling a banana, where the skin separates into four separate pieces.

Let's say that each piece represents the beliefs of a particular religion or nationality, for example:

In Northern Ireland, we have the Catholics and Protestants. In Pakistan, we have the Hindus and Muslims. In Croatia, we have the Catholics and Muslims. For thousands of years, they have been killing each other over the differences in their peels.

They focus their attention on the differences in their peels and ignore the beauty and power of the banana, spirituality.

In our Twelve Step Program, we don't focus on the *skins*. We focus on the *banana.* This is where we gain access to the Power that transforms our:

Fears to courage,
Anger to peace,
Resentments to forgiveness,
Self-pity to gratitude, and
Lust to intimacy.

THE EMPTY CUP

The emptiness in a cup is what makes it useful for drinking. In our attempt to understand the difference between spiritually and religion, we don't begin by adding new ideas and information.

We begin by "emptying" our mind of all the preconceived ideas and beliefs we have on this topic.

Being open minded is a crucial first step for exploring the ways that spiritual principles can enrich our lives. A good place to start is by reading the chapter, WE AGNOSTICS, in the book **Alcoholics Anonymous**.

Leaving our comfort zones and letting go of old, negative beliefs, habits, and ideas requires resolve and courage. It opens the door to having the essential spiritual experience that is so vital for our recovery.

Most members of Alcoholics Anonymous regard the Big Book as the "Bible" of recovery. But we consistently ignore the wisdom and experience contained in the book. Not one word in the basic text has ever been changed, or will ever be changed, because of the **power** contained in the message.

Unfortunately the verbal messages being carried to newcomers in the rooms of A.A. and N.A. have gone through some dramatic changes. However, you won't find any of these "messages" in our recovery literature.

Instead of asking a newcomer to *stretch their mind*, and consider the "possibility" that they just may have a spiritual force and power inside them that is *much more powerful* than their addiction, we often tell them to *shrink their minds* and tell them they can use their tooth brush as their "higher" power.

We're afraid to tell them the truth, that they have a terminal disease which, left untreated, will result in a lot more mental, emotional, spiritual, and physical pain as well as chronic relapses, jails, institutions, or death.

Maybe the recovery rate would be much higher if we followed the directions given to us by the original members of A.A.

"We needed to ask ourselves, but one short question.

'Do I now believe, or am I even willing to believe that there is a Power greater than myself?'

'As soon as a man says he does believe, or is willing to believe, we emphatically assure him that he is on his way. It has repeatedly proven among us that upon this simple cornerstone a wonderfully effective spiritual structure can be built." (A.A. P 47)

A **cornerstone** is something that is essential, indispensable, or basic. What wonderful effective spiritual structure can be built on the sands of empty shoe boxes and doorknobs?

Before we can come to believe that a Power greater than ourselves can restore us to sanity, we must understand the source of our insanity. Our *habit* becomes our obsession. Now add compulsions and cravings.

When you add these three together you not only end up with a lunatic, but a lunatic with a mission. You have someone who is willing to do "whatever it takes" to get more pills, alcohol, or drugs. Webster's dictionary defines sanity as:

a. Free from mental derangement.
b. Having a sound, healthy mind, capable of reasoning; using sound judgment and good sense.

> Are we being sane, using "sound judgment and good sense," when we tell newcomers they don't need to believe in a Power greater than themselves to recover their sanity; that they can use dead batteries as their "Higher" Power, because that's exactly what we are telling them.

To gain more insight and understanding into what a "higher" power is, let's again look at the definition of power.

POWER: Strength, might, or force. The ability to do or act, capable of accomplishing something.

What *strength, might, or force* will newcomers find in dull, dead, lifeless, spiritless objects which **lack the power or force** of living things, objects which have no innate ability to accomplish anything?

When we tell newcomers to use inanimate objects as their *Higher Power*, are we literally "killing them" with kindness because we're afraid they may not stay around if we tell them the truth; that the solution we offer is a spiritual solution.

Should we, at least, use *sound judgment and good sense*, and tell newcomers to use **living things** as their "higher" power:

1. The A.A. or N.A. Group is a "higher" power.
2. Nature: Sunrises, sunsets, and oceans are "higher" powers.
3. Art: Poems, music, or movies that evoke a feeling of awe are "higher" powers.

Unlike us, the original members of A.A. used common sense by telling newcomers who had a problem with "God" to use the group as a Higher Power.

In order to find the answer to this "God" question, the first thing we have to do is stop playing God.

In other words, we have to stop trying to make our spouse, partner, children, parents, and friends in our own image and likeness.

Before any of us can come to believe that a Power "greater' than ourselves can restore us to sanity, we must find our own answers to four basic questions:

1. Do I believe that God exists; that there is a Power, a strength, might, or force that can help me become an addiction survivor?
2. If God exists, does He listen to me?
3. If God listens to me, does that mean He will answer all my prayers?
4. If there is a loving God who speaks and listens to me, then why is there so much pain and suffering in the world?

- Kelly -

HEY GOD! ARE YOU LISTENING?

Hey God!
I owe a lot of money.
The debts are coming due.
I am running out of time.
I am really in a stew.
Hey God, are you listening?

I need to find a job.
I need to pay the rent.
The landlord's coming over.
And I don't have a cent.
Hey God, are you listening?

My family's given up.
They don't know what to think.
My life is in a shambles.
I really need a drink.
Hey God, are you listening?

If you would send some money
I'd turn my life around.
I'd live my life for others.
I'd tell them what I found.
Hey God, are you listening?

I promise I'll reform
If you'll help me with this jam.
I'll walk the straight and narrow.
I'll be your biggest fan.
Hey God, are you listening?

Hey Man!
Don't blame me for your problems.
Don't blame me for your past.

- Radical Recovery -

It wasn't I who swallowed the pills.
It wasn't I who emptied the glass.
Hey man, are you listening?

I've always been beside you
To raise you when you fell.
I kept offering heaven.
But you kept choosing hell.
Hey man, are you listening?

I see the void within your soul;
The pain behind your eyes.
I know the heavy heart you bear.
I can hear it in your sighs.
Hey man, are you listening?

There is a bridge that you must cross
Which separates fact from fiction.
The bridge is called denial.
The fact is your addiction.
Hey man, are you listening?

I can't be there in person
To walk with you each day.
But if you'll just take the Steps
I promise – I'll light the way.
Hey man, are you listening?

GOD SAID "NO!"

I asked God to take away my addiction.
God said: "No!"
That's something you have to give Me.
Are you ready to *reach out*, take My hand, and
Walk the *Twelve Steps* that will lead you to freedom?
Are you willing to be filled with a new craving,
A craving for truth, humility, compassion, gratitude, honesty,
tolerance, forgiveness, intimacy, peace, and solitude?
I asked God to take away my fears.
God said: "No!"
I don't take away.
I give.
Ask Me for courage
So you may face and overcome your fears.
I asked God to grant me patience.
God said: "No!"
Patience comes from trust.
When you begin to trust Me,
Then you will have the patience of the sun, moon, and tides
Which rise and fall in perfect harmony
Every day.
I asked God to give me happiness.
God said: "No!"
You confuse pleasure with happiness.
Happiness comes from
Loving and *serving* others.
I asked God to spare me pain.
God said: "No!"
I gave you pain as a teacher
To let you know you are moving in the wrong direction.
Would you have turned to Me if you weren't in pain?
I asked God to make my spirit grow.
God said" "No!"
Your busy mind keeps getting in the way.

Sit and listen.
You don't even have to listen.
Simply sit and wait.
You don't even have to wait.
Just *practice* being still, and *know* that I am God.
Enter the cocoon of silence.
Then, my *Spirit* will flow into you
As a river flows into the ocean.
I asked God for all things that I might enjoy life.
God said: "No."
You have the habit of getting things backward.
Stop loving things and using people.
Start using things and loving people,
Then your life will be filled with joy.
I asked God to forgive me for all the wrongs I have done.
God said: "No!"
You keep asking the wrong questions.
My forgiveness is constant, like the sun.
Ask Me to help you forgive yourself
For being human.
Ask Me to help you accept
The good, bad, beautiful, and ugly
Parts of your Life
As your training ground for
Creating a heart filled with great compassion.

WHY DOES GOD ALLOW PAIN AND SUFFERING?

A woman went to a beauty salon to have her hair cut. As the stylist began to cut her hair, they began to have a pleasant conversation.

They talked about the economy, changing weather patterns, and the billions of dollars politicians spend degrading each other on television adds.

Eventually, they touched on the subject of religion.

The stylist said: "I don't believe God exists."

The woman asked, "Why do you say that?"

"Well, all you have to do is watch the evening news to know that God doesn't exist.

- *Kelly* -

Tell me, if God existed:
Would there be abandoned and abused children?
Would there be wars?
Would there be homeless people?
Would there be millions of alcoholics and drug addicts?
Would there be sexual predators?
I can't imagine a loving God who would allow these terrible things to happen."
The woman thought for a moment, but didn't respond because she didn't want to get into an argument.
The stylist finished cutting the woman's hair, and the woman left the shop.
As she left the beauty salon she saw a woman standing by a bus stop. Her hair was long, knotted, and looked like it needed a good washing.
The woman came back to the beauty salon, looked at the stylist, and said:
"You know what? Hair stylists don't exist."
"How can you say that" asked the surprised stylist?
"I am here, and I am a hair stylist, and I just cut your hair."
"No!" the woman replied.
"Hair stylists don't exist because if they did, there wouldn't be women like the girl standing by the bus stop."
"Ah, but hair stylists do exist!
The problem is that people *choose* not to come to me."
"Exactly!" affirmed the woman.
"That's the point! God also does exist!
The problem is that people have free will, and *choose* not to look for Him, or come to Him.
That's why there's so much pain and suffering in the world."
Perhaps the best way to understand the *process* it takes to transform our cravings for pills, alcohol, and drugs into cravings for freedom, honesty, compassion, integrity, humility, and peace is to understand:

WHY BUTTERFLIES ARE FREE

The caterpillar squirmed, wormed, and
    wiggled its way through
    the darkness of the night.

He was tired, tired of searching for *something*
that would fill the void he felt *Inside*.

He had indulged his senses in every earthly pleasure.

He had sculptured his body to perfection,

He had accumulated a wealth of insects

That was the envy of the caterpillar kingdom.

He was admired and respected by the
elite of his community, but none of these
accomplishments satisfied him.

There was always a need for *more*.

Life was a maze with no way out. There were
    no avenues left to explore.

He prayed to an *unknown* God for an end

to his earthly existence.

From out of the darkness a ray of light
    appeared through the top of a nearby tree.

Dawn!

He heard an inner voice.

"*Climb, climb the tree.*"

He had nothing to lose. He faced complete
destruction, or maybe, one more attempt at
peace.

He climbed all day to reach the top.

One last lunge, butterflies, thousands of them. But
why? Suddenly, he knew.

- Kelly -

An ugly caterpillar, a beautiful butterfly, but how?

Then he saw it, the cocoon. He watched as a butterfly emerged fluttering its wings.

Awakening, he surrendered to the Power within his earthly frame.

He let go of all his illusions about who and what he thought he was.

He knew why butterflies are free.

MYTH 5

JUST DON'T PICK UP

"Results, specific and measurable, come from having a clear vision, defining what improvement and adaptation looks like, and having a beginning and an end in mind." (Vince Lombardi)

R EMEMBER THE STORY ABOUT THE three little pigs?
It provides a great lesson.

It tells us what we need to do to get "anchored" in our recovery.

An anchor is a person or thing that can be relied on for support, stability, and security.

THE HOUSE OF STRAW

You build a house of straw when you think you can stay clean and sober by "just not picking up" a pill, drink, or drug. You never ask the question:

WHERE do I get the Power to "just not pick up?"

When the winds of fear, anger, resentment, guilt, shame, and boredom hit the house of straw, it gets blown away by these powerful emotions.

THE HOUSE OF TWIGS

You build a house of twigs when you think you can stay "sober" by just not picking up a pill, drink, or drug, and going to meetings. There's no "cement" holding the twigs together.

When the hurricanes come, and they will, you lose a job, career, or your home, someone you love dies, you are served with divorce papers, or lose custody of your children, etc., the house of twigs gets *blown away* by the winds of depression, self- pity, anxiety, and despair.

THE HOUSE OF BRICK

You build a house of brick when use "anchors," people or things that you can rely on for support, stability, and security.

When the winds and hurricanes come along, you *stand strong* in the face of these powerful forces because you're recovery is anchored in the Twelve Steps. Let's put this in perspective.

There's a legend about an American Indian who, while hunting, came across an eagle's egg. He wandered around the woods for hours, looking for an eagle's nest, but couldn't find one. What he did find, was a hen, sitting in her nest, surrounded by a bunch of chickens. So, he put the eagle's egg in the hen's nest. Two days later, this baby eagle emerged from its shell. He looked around, saw the chickens,

and started to do what chickens do, peck at seeds, and flutter around the hen. He did this his whole life. He was totally unaware of the extraordinary powers Nature had bestowed on him:
- His ability to fly above the large, confining mountains that surrounded him.
- The power of his wings.
- The awe and ecstasy he could have experienced gliding high above the earth.

Then one day an eagle flew over the field of chickens. The now aging eagle, who, because of his size had been told, and believed, that he was a deformed chicken, looked up in awe at the great bird soaring across the sky.

"What is that?" he asked one of the elder chickens.

The elder chicken replied, "That is an eagle. I have never seen one up close, but it is the proudest, most magnificent, and most inspiring of all birds. If I could be anything I wanted to be, it would definitely be an eagle."

Then, the elder chicken noticed a sparkle in the eyes of his companion. Looking deep inside those sparkling eyes, he said,

"But don't you ever get the idea that you can be an eagle. You're just a deformed chicken. That's all you have ever been, and it's all you ever will be."

Shackled by this belief, the eagle lived and died thinking he was a deformed chicken.

What's the moral of this story? If you want to become an addiction survivor, you have to:

ONE: Stop hanging around with chickens.

TWO: Go to Eagle School, where you will learn how to S.O.A.R.

Step out of your comfort zone and begin developing the extraordinary powers that Nature has bestowed on you.

Open your mind.

Accept the good, bad, beautiful, and ugly parts of yourself, and the "lessons" you needed to learn.

Recover mentally, emotionally, spiritually, and physically.

THREE: Remove all the limiting labels you have put on yourself, or that someone else has put on you.

Now, in the world of recovery, we have eagles, and we have chickens. How can you tell if you are an eagle or a chicken?

CHICKENS: They want all the "promises" that come with recovery, but they aren't willing to do the work it takes to make those promises come true.

EAGLES: They want all the "promises" of recovery, but they are willing to make the sacrifices, and do the work it takes to make those promises come true, and to continue practicing the *Maintenance Steps* as a way of life.

Are you a chicken or an eagle?

YOUR BODY

In case you didn't know, if you are an alcoholic or drug addict, you have an "abnormal" body.

This abnormality makes you, me, and every other alcoholic and drug addict on the planet *different* from other people.

"We who have suffered alcoholic torture must believe that the body of the alcoholic is quite as abnormal as his mind." *(A.A. P xxvi)*

WHAT MAKES OUR BODIES ABNORMAL?

"The doctor's theory that we have an allergy to alcohol interests us. As laymen, our opinion as to its soundness may, of course, mean little. But as ex-problem drinkers we can say that his explanation makes sense." *(A.A. Page xxvi)*

al·ler·gy: An abnormal reaction of the body to a substance or allergen introduced by inhalation, ingestion, or injection.

THE ALLERGY

"One symptom alcoholics have in common: They cannot start drinking without developing the phenomenon of craving. This extraordinary phenomenon, as we have suggested, may be the manifestation of an allergy which differentiates these people and sets them apart as a distinct entity. It has never been, by any treatment with which we are familiar, permanently eradicated. The only relief we have to suggest is entire abstinence." *(A.A. Page xxx)*

"WE ADMITTED WE WERE POWERLESS OVER ALCOHOL."

The term powerless relates specifically to our abnormal bodies, the *allergy* we have to the mood altering substances we put inside our bodies, the *allergy* that differentiates us from other people, the *allergy* that sets us apart as a distinct entity, the *allergy* that creates tidal waves of insatiable cravings that we can't control "after" we put alcohol or drugs inside our bodies.

The term *powerless*, as it relates to us as alcoholics and drug addicts, does not apply to our mind, emotions, or behavior. Why not? Because:

We are not *powerless* over the way we think.
We are not *powerless* over the way we feel.
We are not *powerless* over the way we act.

Some people have an *allergic* reaction to certain foods or pollens. We happen to have an *allergic* reaction to the **chemicals** in alcohol and drugs.

There is nothing we can do to make this *allergy* go away. This is what we are powerless over - our "allergic" reaction to the **chemicals** in pills, alcohol, and drugs. Until the day we die, the *allergy* will sit inside our bodies, like a dormant volcano. But it's really quite harmless, so long as we don't put anything inside our body that will make the volcano erupt.

WHAT MAKES THE VOLCANO ERUPT?

When we pop a few Oxy's, Vicodin, Percocet, or Xanax, have a few beers, snort some cocaine, or shoot up with heroin, we have an *allergic* reaction. The volcano erupts.

It unleashes a tidal wave of insatiable cravings we can't control. Our brain gets hijacked, and we get cut off from all access to:

1. Rational Thought: "I could go to prison, lose my job, career, marriage, driver's license, custody of my children, etc."
2. When the tidal wave of cravings flood our brain, we don't have access to the memory of what happened the last time we forgot that we had an *allergy* to the chemicals in alcohol and drugs.

3. Love is the *second* most powerful force in the universe. The *first*, and most powerful force in the universe is cravings because "after" we put the pills, alcohol or drugs inside our bodies, the volcano erupts. We then lose all access to the love we have for our parents, spouse, partner, children, and the promise we made: "I love you. I promise, I'll never do it again."

It's a battle we can't win. Why can't we win the battle? *Because, it's not a fair fight.* For us, pills, alcohol, and drugs are similar to Ex-Lax. We only become powerless AFTER we put these substances inside our bodies.

Over the last 30 years, a new breed of alcoholics and drug addicts have come up with what appears to be an easier and softer way of helping newcomers get started on their recovery journey. All a newcomer has to do is, *"Just don't pick up - no matter what."*

Try using this approach the next time you want to smoke a cigarette. The problem with this easier and softer way is that it doesn't work because "We are without defense against the first drink." *(A.A. Page 24).*

What "worked" for the original members of A.A?

"When we were approached by those in whom the problem had been solved, there was nothing left for us to do but pick up the simple kit of spiritual tools laid at our feet." *(A.A. Page 25)*

The original members of A.A. had a very high recovery rate. Today, by comparison, we have a very high relapse rate. Perhaps it would be in our best interest, as alcoholics and addicts, to go back to the philosophy of: "If it works, don't fix it." The "Just don't pick up" approach ignores the dilemma we face as alcoholics and drug addicts:

"Lack of power - that was our dilemma." *(A.A. Page 45)*

What *power* did the original members of A.A. lack? They **lacked the power** to *just not pick up a pill, drink or drug,* because the "habit" they once had, was no longer a habit. It had become an obsession and compulsion. They were compelled to drink or use drugs. They didn't have a choice. What was an option for them was being "willing" to soar like an eagle, to go to any lengths to achieve **victory** over their addiction, and this they did. To give newcomers *hope,* maybe more A.A. meetings should begin with:

"The problem has been removed. It does not exist for us. We are neither cocky, nor are we afraid. This is our experience. That is how we react so long as we stay in fit spiritual condition." (A.A. Page 85)

Now, using a radical approach to recovery, I am going to suggest that you *stretch your mind,* that you begin developing the extra-ordinary powers that Nature has bestowed on you, and that you be *willing* to consider the possibility that you just might have a Spiritual Force and Power inside you that is *much more powerful* than your addiction, *much more powerful* than the obsessive thoughts, compulsive feelings, and physical cravings that control and dominate your life.

I am not going to suggest that you *shrink your mind* by telling you to believe that "inanimate" objects can provide you with the faith, courage, strength, inspiration, and motivation you need to become free from the slavery of addiction. Why not?

A healthy dose of common sense would indicate that telling you to use inanimate objects as a "higher power," is bad advice. And we wonder why the relapse rate is so high. Today, one of the main problems with recovery, is recovery. Using another radical approach to recovery, I am going to suggest that you get **in** instead of **out** of the driver's seat.

WHAT'S THE DIFFERENCE?

With recovery, we get **in** the driver's seat by asking for help, guidance, and direction as we begin our recovery journey. We take responsibility for our past and future by learning how to change the way we think, feel, and act. We follow the map and directions laid out for us by the original members of A.A. Now, one of the things I am **not** going to suggest is that you ask God to become your "chauffeur." Why not?

To become addiction survivors, we have to deal with reality, not illusions. There should be no doubt in the mind of any alcoholic or drug addict that we got **out** of the driver's seat the day we became addicted to pills, alcohol, or drugs, and became classic examples of "self-will run riot."

For many of us, life was like walking through a minefield, always anxious, always fearful, always anticipating the next explosion.

Each of us should be able to recognize that long before we attended our first meeting we were out of control. So, perhaps we should stop telling newcomers to get "out" of the driver's seat because when erratic emotions and physical cravings control our lives, we are not **in** the driver's seat

The Twelve Steps are designed to help us "wash our brains;" not "brainwash" us into believing myths that consistently fail to pass the common sense test like , "Our disease is doing pushups."

Our disease is doing pushups.

Our disease is cunning, baffling, and powerful.

Our disease doesn't have to do pushups.

We are the ones who have to do the pushups by developing our spiritual muscle, which *is much more powerful* than our addiction.

How do we develop our spiritual muscle?

We *practice* the *Maintenance Steps, 10, 11, 12* on a daily basis.

Here's a large dose of common sense.

You don't have to complete Steps 1 through 9 before you can begin taking an inventory of your day, pray, meditate, or help another alcoholic or addict. You can start the *Maintenance Steps* the day you walk into treatment.

Let's pause here for a moment to consider a critical point we must understand, if we want to become free from the slavery of addiction.

If we don't understand this critical point, we will never have a future. What we will have is a past – a past that will keep repeating itself, over and over again.

The critical point we must understand is the difference between powerless and power.

POWERLESS

Again, this term *specifically* relates to our body, the "allergy," the dormant volcano sitting inside our body. There is nothing we can do about the *allergic* reaction we have to the **chemicals** in pills, alcohol and drugs once we put them *inside* our body. This is what we are **powerless** over If we don't put them *inside* our body, we don't become powerless.

LACK OF POWER

Upon arriving at the doors of A.A. or N.A., we *lack the power* to "control" the obsessive thoughts, compulsive feelings, and physical cravings that dominate our lives. Unlike the *allergy*, there is something we can do about this. We can take the Twelve Steps that will give us access to the Power we need to "tame" the obsessive thoughts, compulsive feelings, and physical cravings that create so much pain and suffering in our lives, and the lives of those we love.

"LACK OF POWER - THAT WAS OUR DILEMMA"

The "dilemma" represents the parts of our lives that need healing: our mind, emotions, and spirit.

MIND: "The main problem centers in the mind." *(A.A. Page 27)*

EMOTIONS: "By discovering what our emotional deformities are, we can move toward their correction." *(12 Steps and 12 Traditions, Page 43)*

SPIRIT: "When the spiritual malady is overcome, we straighten out mentally and physically." *(A.A. Page 64)*

Bill Wilson defined addiction as, "*A cancer of the emotions and soul.*"

If we want to heal this cancer of the emotions and the soul, we need to do more than just not drink or use drugs and go to meetings. As stated earlier, we must be willing to treat what the medical profession calls, *The Disease of Chemical Dependency*, with the same passion, fervor, and desperation as someone who is diagnosed with cancer, because again, addiction, like cancer, when it is left untreated, is a *terminal* disease. Each year, at least one famous person reminds us about the fatal aspect of our disease.

If you are willing to **S.O.A.R** like an eagle and practice the twelve spiritual principles in the Steps, as a way of life, you will discover that you are power-full. Like the seed planted in the ground, you will awaken a Spiritual Power and Force inside you that is *much more powerful* than your addiction, *much more powerful* than the obsessive thoughts, compulsive feelings and physical cravings that make your life unmanageable.

Knowing what we are powerless over is the first baby step in recovery.

This begs the question: If we can "recover," why is the relapse rate so high? There are several obvious reasons.

FIRST: WE DON'T BELIEVE THE TRUTHS WE HEAR

We hear these "truths" every time we attend an A.A. meeting. However, it is much less frightening and challenging to accept *myths* instead of *truths*.

When these "myths" come under the microscope of common sense, they consistently fail the test, but that doesn't seem to bother us very much.

WHAT IS THE TRUTH?

The "truth" comes to us in the form of three very pertinent ideas:
(a) That we were alcoholic and could not manage our own lives.
(b) That probably no human power (or inanimate object) could have relieved our alcoholism.
(c) That God could and would if He were sought. *(A.A. Page 60)*
But most of us deny, dismiss, or just don't believe these truths. For some reason, we prefer to believe that God **can't** or **won't** relieve us of the obsessive thoughts, compulsive feelings, and physical cravings that come with the "package" of addiction; that the "fight" with alcohol and drugs will continue until the day we die, that the promise of "a new freedom" is the real myth of recovery.

While we may be willing to go to any lengths to avoid picking up our drug of choice, apparently we are not willing to go to any lengths to achieve **victory** over our addiction. We are not willing to go to any lengths to **find a spiritual experience** which is defined as: "A personality change sufficient to bring about recovery from alcoholism." *(A.A. Page 567).*

Since 1935, when A.A. was founded, the *Recovery Power Mindset* passed on to us by the original members of A.A. has, for the most part, disappeared. It has been replaced with the *Recovery Powerless Mindset*.

SECOND: WE CHOOSE TO BELIEVE MYTHS INSTEAD OF TRUTHS

"We of Alcoholics Anonymous are more than one hundred men and women who have recovered from a seemingly hopeless state of mind and body." *(A.A. Page xiii)*

The "truth" seems very clear.

The original members of A.A. *recovered* from a seemingly hopeless state of mind and body.

They achieved victory over alcohol.

The problem was removed.

The problem didn't exist for them, and it didn't come back - so long as they stayed in fit spiritual condition.

In the rooms of A.A. and N.A. many people say they are "recovering."

This is true for them.

Why?

Because whatever kind of spiritual awakening they may have had, it obviously wasn't powerful enough to help them achieve **victory** over alcohol or drugs, or to create "a **personality change** sufficient enough to bring about **recovery** from alcoholism."

But it doesn't have to be this way.

We have a choice.

We can choose **OLD A.A.** or **NEW A.A.**

OLD A.A: "Came to believe that a Power greater than ourselves could restore us to sanity." *(A.A. Page 45)*

NEW A.A: Came to believe that a power **less than ourselves** could restore us to sanity. (Doorknobs, chairs, toilet paper, etc.)

OLD A.A: "Remind the prospect that their recovery is not dependent upon people. It is dependent upon their relationship with God." *(A.A. Page 99)*

NEW A.A: Remind the prospect that their recovery **is** dependent upon people. "Meeting makers make it."

OLD A.A: "The problem has been removed. It does not exist for us." *(A.A. Page 85)*

NEW A.A: The problem will never be removed. We will never achieve **victory** over our addiction.

OLD A.A: "We have decided to go to any lengths to find a spiritual experience." *(A.A. Page 79)*

NEW A.A: We have decided to go to any lengths to avoid picking up a pill, drink, or drug.

MYTH 6

ALCOHOL AND DRUGS MAKE OUR LIVES UNMANAGEABLE

"Self-importance is our greatest enemy. Think about it - what weakens us is feeling offended by the deeds and misdeeds of our fellowmen. Our self-importance requires that we spend most of our lives offended by someone." (Carlos Castaneda)

T HE BELIEF THAT ALCOHOL AND drugs make our lives unmanageable is a common belief in A.A. and N.A. But this is not true.

We don't need alcohol or drugs to make our lives unmanageable. We are quite capable of doing that all on our own. Alcohol and drugs make our lives **more** unmanageable.

When an alcoholic or addict picks up a pill, drink, or a drug, it's like someone throwing gasoline on a house that's already on fire. The added "fuel" just increases the *intensity* of the flames, and causes a lot more damage.

The original members of A.A. understood this.

"Our liquor was but a symptom." *(A.A. P 64)*

"SELF manifested in various ways was what defeated us." *(A.A. Page 64)*

What are some of the various ways this SELF defeated them? The same way SELF defeated us.

They even came up with a prayer to help them get rid of this SELF that was defeating them.

"Relieve me of the bondage of self, that I may better do Thy will."

What Is The SELF That Keeps Us In Bondage?

Before we can answer this question, we must first understand the "package" we come with as human beings.

Here's the package. It is shaped like a triangle.

                Spirit
                Power

               Cravings
               Desires
    Mind   Emotions
    Thoughts   Feelings

The **SELF** that controls our lives has **five parts**: Body, mind, emotions, spirit, and cravings. This is the "package" we arrive with the day we are born.

BODY

The triangle itself is a symbol for our body.

It's the "vehicle" we use to get around the planet.

There are three points on the triangle.

These are three of the **drivers** "inside" our vehicle: Thoughts, Feelings, and Spirit. Each one of these drivers performs a very important function, for example:

MIND

If you are trying to solve a crossword puzzle, a math problem, or change the electrical wiring in your home, your **mind** needs to be in the driver's seat of your vehicle.

EMOTIONS

If a friend is grieving the loss of a loved one, celebrating the birth of a child, or a promotion at work, your **emotions** need to be in the driver's seat of your vehicle, so you can, through empathy, feel their pain or joy.

SPIRIT

If someone cuts you off in traffic and you feel angry, you can "change drivers" by replacing your anger (emotion) with forgiveness (a spiritual principle.)

CRAVINGS

Our cravings, represent the "passenger" **inside** our vehicle. When this passenger takes control of our vehicle, we lie, we cheat, and we steal, time or money, from those who love us. We run over *anyone* who gets in the way of our getting drugs or alcohol. We miss birthday parties, anniversaries, work, our children's events at school, etc.

Why can't we win this battle?
Because, it's not a fair fight.
Our human resources, our mind, spirit, and emotions are no match for the cravings which turn into giant Tsunamis; leaving a wake of destruction in their path.

These five parts**:** body, mind, emotions, spirit, and cravings are the various *parts* that make the *whole*, the **SELF**.

PHYSICAL CRAVINGS

They blind us, cut us off from our spirit, emotions, and our ability to think rationally.

EMOTIONS

Negative emotions can flood the entire space inside our vehicle: Fear, rage, anger, guilt, shame, self-pity, boredom, jealousy, etc.

These negative emotions have the effect of drowning our mind and spirit.

They turn us into *victims* of the powerful negative forces that begin to "control" our lives.

MIND

The **ON** button in our mind can get "stuck," where we can't shut it off. When this happens, thousands of thoughts race through our mind uncontrollably, every day, like a herd of wild horses. Our mind goes where it wants to go, and does what it wants to do, even while we sleep.

This continuous racing of our mind has the effect of *smothering* our emotions and spirit.

In order to identify the SELF that keeps us in bondage, we have to identify the *root cause* of the unmanageability in our lives.

Does the unmanageability in our lives originate *inside* or *outside* our vehicle?

Do we blame money, people, events, substances, or situations for making our lives unmanageable, or is the unmanageability in our lives based on the way we *think* and *feel* about money, and the people, events, substances, or situations in our lives?

Treating a "symptom" of a disease, never heals the disease. To be relieved of the bondage of SELF, we need to stop focusing our attention "outside" ourselves, on the *symptom*. We need to draw our attention "inward."

Buddha nailed this on the head more than twenty-five hundred years ago when he made the discovery that all the suffering and unmanageability in his life came from what he called THE THREE POISONS:
   1. Delusional Thinking

2. Destructive Emotions, and
3. Physical Cravings

DELUSIONAL THINKING

It dawned on me one day that the reason I drank and used drugs was because I was lonely. What I needed to overcome my loneliness, and be happy, was the right woman in my life. With the right woman, my loneliness would disappear, and I would be so happy. Finally, I found her, and two months later I was saying, "If I could just get rid of her, I would be so happy."

I had grown up Catholic, but by the time I arrived at A.A., I had lost all belief in God. One Sunday morning, I turned on the television and a minister said, "God loves you, and God wants you to be happy."

I thought I may as well give the God thing one more shot. I knew that if I had money, I would be very happy. Then, surely, I wouldn't want to drink or use drugs. So, I went to a convenience store and bought a lottery ticket. The payout was $70 million.

There was a church up the street from where I lived, and I made a deal with God, if He existed, that I would split the winnings 50-50. I was sure the church could use the money, and both the church and I, would do wonderful things with it.

Didn't get one number!

This reinforced my belief that God did not exist, but I now know that, had I won the lottery, I wouldn't have written this book. I would have drank enough alcohol, or used enough drugs where I would have ended up joining the ranks of all the rich and famous people who died from their addiction to pills, alcohol, or drugs.

Delusional thinking comes in many forms.

Perhaps the most common one is that there is some "person" or "thing" out there that will fix me and make me happy.

What I learned, as I made progress in my recovery journey, is that happiness is an inside job.

Having delusional thoughts, about what will make us happy, shows up in many areas of our lives.

If I had... a bigger house.
If I had... a better job.
If I had... that beautiful car.

If I had... a better looking body.
If I had... more or better sex.
If I had... more respect from people.

Many of us get the *things* that we think will make us happy, but the novelty soon wears off, and we're back looking for **more** of something else that will make us happy.

CRAVINGS
How Do We Become "Chemically" Dependent?

Imagine you're a car battery.

For years, you function just the way a car battery is supposed to function.

Then one day, you just can't get going, and you get to experience your first "jump start."

When that "juice" starts to flow through you, you say something like.

"Oh my God!"

"Oh my God! "

"This feels so good. Where has the *cable man* been all my life?"

From that day forward, you "want" a jump start every day.

And you do this for years.

Then one day, the "cable man" doesn't show up, and you learn something new about yourself.

You no longer "want" a jump start.

You "need" a jump start.

Without that *jump start*, you don't feel normal.

You have lost the ability to feel good on your own.

You are now "dependent" on the cable man to make you feel good, and one jump start just doesn't do it anymore.

You now need a 12 pack of jump starts just to make it through the day. Sound familiar?

Can you relate?

With alcohol and drugs, what starts out as a wonderful love affair that gives us lots of pleasure, becomes an abusive relationship.

The desire for pleasure gets replaced by the *need* to avoid the pain of withdrawal, and we only have one coping skill to deal with that pain.

We pick up a pill, drink, or drug.

There are more than 150 Twelve Step Programs. Just one word separates us from each other:
We admitted we were powerless over_____
However, we all have the same *primary* addiction.
When we experience DIS-EASE, anxiety, fear, resentment, anger, guilt, shame, boredom, despair, depression, loneliness, etc., what's the first thing we want to do?
We want to get rid of our DIS-EASE by creating a mood altering experience.
How do we create a mood altering experience? Some of us gamble, on line or at the Casino, to create this mood altering experience – Gamblers Anonymous.
For some of us it's food – Overeaters Anonymous.
For others it may be promiscuous sex, or porno web sites: Sex Addicts Anonymous, Cyber Sex Anonymous.
But for most of us, it's a lot simpler. We simply pick up a pill, drink, or drug to get rid of our *dis-ease*.
One of the chains that keeps us in bondage is cravings. In other words, it's not the substance that keeps us in bondage, but the *craving* for the substance.

WHY DO WE CRAVE THE SUBSTANCE?

1. It provides us with instant gratification.
2. It's a habit, a coping skill we have developed for dealing with the *dis-ease* of everyday life.
3. It is comfortable and familiar.

The poem, CHANGE, may give us some insight into the dilemma we face.

CHANGE

Each day the sun rises and the sun sets.
The tide comes in and the tide goes out.
Each dawn darkness yields to morning's light.

Each year winter's barren branches bloom
With buds of spring;
Summer greens give way to
Autumn reds and yellows.

We live in a universal womb
Where change
Is a natural and constant factor.

Every womb has a birth canal
Where the rite of passage
Requires
A complete surrender
To a process of transformation.

When this surrender occurs
The caterpillar... emerges as a butterfly;
The seed... emerges as a flower;
The body... emerges as a spirit.

Change
Is neither positive nor negative.
It's our
Resistance to change
That is positive or negative.

MYTH 7

MEETING MAKERS MAKE IT

"All men's miseries derive from not being able to sit, alone and quiet, for twenty minutes." (Blaise Pascal)

M**Y SOBRIETY DATE IS OCTOBER 8, 1975.** During my first twenty years, I was a "meeting maker." I made five meetings a week. My motivation for attending meetings was based on two factors, fear and greed.

GREED: I wanted to make money, and I knew that if I drank or used drugs, that wasn't going to happen.

FEAR: I also knew that if I drank or used drugs it would take me back, mentally and emotionally, to a place I didn't want to go, going to bed at night and praying that I wouldn't wake up in the morning.

I arrived at meetings right before they started, and I left as soon as they were over. I went through the motions of getting a sponsor and working through the Twelve Steps, but I never applied what I learned.

I looked - but I didn't see.
I heard - but I didn't listen.
I touched - but I didn't feel
I read - but I didn't understand.

I really believed that that our Twelve Step program was all about ME just not picking up a drink or a drug. This was reinforced at many of the meetings I attended, where the mantra was, "Meeting makers make it." I couldn't stand Big Book Thumpers.

The combination of meetings, fear, and greed enabled me to "make it" for twenty years. But I was nothing more than a dry drunk; no spiritual awakening, no personality change.

In our literature it states, "We practice all Twelve Steps of the program in our daily lives so that we, and those about us, may find emotional sobriety." I surely didn't "make it" in that area.

In my twentieth year of sobriety, I moved to a place where there was one meeting. It was held at 7 PM every night. It was a very small group, eight people. I liked them. After a month of attending these meetings, something happened. I don't know that I would call it a spiritual experience, but it was certainly a major shift in consciousness.

My motivation for attending meetings changed. I went to meetings to support the other eight people who were there to support me. The lesson I learned was this:

Recovery is not about you. It's not about me. It's about us, supporting and encouraging each other *get* and *stay* sober in the fullest sense of the word; become:

"*Well balanced, realistic, sensible, dignified, rational; not driven to extremes in emotion or thought.*"

One of the primary responsibilities we have as members of Alcoholics Anonymous, Narcotics Anonymous, or any other 12 Step program is to *carry the message* to the newcomer.

This is easier said than done.

If you have ever participated in a communication workshop with twenty or more people, where one person whispered a message to someone else, and that person in turn whispered the message to the next person, you would have witnessed the distortion that took place as each person filtered the message through the lens of their own mind.

"John lost his insurance job, and his wife left him," could end up being "John's wife ran off with their insurance agent."

Can you imagine the distortion that would take place if a message was passed on to millions of people?

At many meetings, "Meeting makers make it," seems to be one of the primary messages that is being carried to newcomers.

At the time the book *Alcoholics Anonymous* was published, everyone was a newcomer. Fortunately, the one hundred original members of A.A. put their "message" in writing. As a matter of fact, a whole chapter of the book, *Working With Others*, provides very clear-cut directions on how to help newcomers get started on their road to recovery.

So, let's go back to the source, let's go back to the "first whisper" to see if the message we are carrying today is consistent with the "message" entrusted to our care by the one hundred original members of A.A.

Let's begin by asking this question: *Why do you attend meetings?*

Now, let's compare that with why the original members of A.A. attended meetings.

There are numerous references to this in the book Alcoholics Anonymous:

"We meet frequently so that newcomers may find the *fellowship* they seek." *(A.A. Page 15)*

"In addition to these casual get-togethers, it became customary to set apart one night a week for a meeting to be attended by anyone interested in a spiritual way of life." *(A.A. Page 159)*

I could be wrong, but it appears to me that their *motivation* for attending meetings was based on:
1. The desire for fellowship.
2. The desire to help the newcomer.
3. Interest in a spiritual way of life.

Is that why you go to meetings?
You enjoy the fellowship.
You want to help newcomers.
You are interested in a spiritual way of life.

I fear that, for many of us, the primary motivation for attending meetings is built on a foundation of fear, like mine was, rather than a foundation of love and service to others.

From what I have observed, newcomers are often told to "keep their fears green," not by helping others, but by showing up to find out what happens to people who don't attend meetings.

In essence, they are told to keep their attention focused on *themselves,* on what they need to do to *avoid* picking up a drink or drug so they don't end up homeless, in jail, treatment, or dead.

Has the "first whisper," of being Good Samaritans who offer a message of *hope* to those still trapped in the slavery of addiction been lost?

Have we become parasites who feed off each other's fears and the suffering of newcomers?

In telling newcomers that the reason people relapse is that they stop going to meetings, aren't we telling them that meetings are the "God" that will keep them clean and sober?

Whatever happened to: "PRACTICAL EXPERIENCE shows that nothing will so much insure immunity from drinking as intensive work with other alcoholics." *(A.A. Page 89)*

MEETING MAKERS MAKE IT

When someone says, "Meeting makers make it," what do they mean? That someone stopped drinking or using drugs?

For some, that is exactly what it means, and this is good. Our families, neighbors, and employers, are delighted we are not drinking or using drugs.

The judges in our courts, and the state troopers on our highways, who have to notify loved ones that someone driving under the influence of alcohol or drugs killed their parent, spouse, or child, are also delighted. But there's PHASE II SOBRIETY, emotional sobriety.

Is there a reference point we can turn to, to determine if we have made it? YES!

If you think of the Twelve Steps as a "recipe" for living a clean, sober, useful, and productive life, you will find the answer in the book Alcoholics Anonymous.

12 WAYS TO TELL IF YOU HAVE "MADE IT"

1. You know a new freedom and happiness. T F
2. You don't regret past, nor wish to shut the door on it. T F
3. You comprehend the word serenity. T F
4. You know peace. T F
5. You now see how your experience can benefit others. T F
6. That feeling of uselessness and self-pity has left you. T F
7. You have lost interest in selfish things; gained interest in helping others. T F
8. Self-seeking has slipped away. T F
9. Your whole attitude and outlook on life has changed. T F
10. Fear of people and of economic insecurity has left you. T F
11. You intuitively know how to handle situations which use to baffle you. T F
12. You realize that God has done for you, what you couldn't do for yourself. T F

Well, what do you think?
Have you made it?

BILL WILSON'S SPIRITUAL AWAKENING

For most of us, our "spiritual awakening" is a slow process, much like the metamorphic change that takes place when a caterpillar goes through the "process" of becoming a butterfly. Bill's was sudden and intense.

Have you had a "spiritual awakening?"
Are you spiritually fit?
Have you laid hold of a source of strength you had previously denied yourself?

As a result of my own "spiritual awakening" I have recovered:
I have **recovered** my health.
I have **recovered** my self-respect and self-esteem.
I have **recovered** the core values I lost.
I have **recovered** my integrity.
I have **recovered** my sanity.
I have **recovered** relationships that I had lost in my addiction.
I have **recovered** emotionally.
I have **recovered** from a spiritual bankruptcy, re-established a conscious contact with God, as I understand Him.

Based on the "original" message passed on to us by the first 100 members of A.A., I can say that I have "recovered," in that:
I have ceased fighting anything or anyone, including alcohol.
The problem has been removed.
It no longer exists for me.
I have lost my fear of today, tomorrow and the hereafter; I have been reborn.
I have had a deep and effective spiritual experience which has revolutionized my whole attitude toward life, toward my relationships, and toward God.
In the face of collapse and despair, in the face of the total failure of my human resources, I have found a new power, a new peace, a new happiness, and a new sense of direction.
That feeling of uselessness and self-pity has left me. I have been granted a perfect release from a very obstinate and potentially fatal obsession.

THERE IS ONLY ONE THING I WILL NEVER RECOVER

As an alcoholic and drug addict, there is only one thing I will never recover, and that is the ability to *safely* use any mind altering drug.

Now, having recovered, if I want to stay recovered, I understand that:

- Kelly -

My future sobriety is dependent upon the growth and maintenance of my spiritual condition.

I must "practice" the spiritual principles of the Twelve Steps as a way of life.

To do this, I must first get rid of my:

ILLUSIONS

In climbing the pyramid of technology
We have discovered new worlds;
Worlds which have distanced us
From the *Spring* which nurtures us
From the *Light* which guides us.
A thread has become a web
Spun with illusions
Where we have learned to
Love things and use people.
Pleasure wears the mask of intimacy
Where the ultimate value masquerades as
A lean sculptured body - with a large bank account.

In the dance of life
When the music stops
We may discover that
We are lost and wandering alone
In a desert of spiritual isolation.
To find the path
Which will bring us back
To our Source
of
Nourishment and light
We must walk the wilderness between us, and
Transform it
By gentle and persistent efforts
Into a garden of solitude
Where we can nurture each other
With acts of kindness, unselfishness, and love.

If you haven't "made it," perhaps the story of *The Two Wolves* will provide you with the tools and resources you need to achieve this goal.

THE TWO WOLVES

One evening an old Cherokee Indian told his grandson a story about a battle that goes on inside every human being. He said: "My son, the battle is between two wolves."

ONE IS SORROW

It is *driven* by self-hatred. It is filled with a hundred forms of fear, anger, resentment, guilt, despair, shame, and self-pity. This wolf dwells alone, in isolation, and lives in the **past and the future**. It trusts no one, not God, not others, not even itself. It spends its entire time running back and forth between the past and the future. *It knows no peace.*

ONE IS JOY

It is *driven* by a healthy form of self-love. It is filled with a hundred forms of courage, faith, hope, compassion, humility, patience, and gratitude. This wolf "connects" with other wolves, and shares in their joys and sorrows. It lives in the **present**. This wolf has crossed the bridge of trust, and is guided by the *Great Spirit* which lies within each and every wolf. *It knows peace.*

The grandson thought about it for a minute, then asked his grandfather this question:

"Which wolf wins?"

The old Cherokee simply replied, "The one you feed."

Which one do you want to feed, *Sorrow*, or *Joy*?

If you answered Joy, then you must start feeding Joy the *food* that will help you experience more self-love, courage, faith, hope, compassion, humility, patience, and gratitude.

The food comes in three varieties;
MEDITATION

"Use the light. Come home to your true nature. Don't cause yourself injury: This is known as seizing the truth." (Lao Tsu)

For 10 to 20 minutes a day, practice taming your mind, so you can learn how to *slow down* the racing thoughts and erratic emotions that create so much dis-ease. Learn how to disengage from the past and the future. Listen to CDs such as:

Eliminating Stress, Finding Inner Peace, by Brian Weiss, Anger and Forgiveness, by Belle Ruth Naperstak, Letting Go of Stress, by Emmet Miller, Tuning In, by Cheryl Richardson, Grief, Anger and Forgiveness, by Stephen and Andrea Levine, Guided Meditations: For Calmness, Awareness, and Love, by Bodhipaksa

REFLECTION

You can't solve a problem with the same mind that created it. (Albert Einstein)

Your mind, like your body, needs nourishing food.

Turn your car into a classroom. Listen to CD's such as:

The Four Agreements, by Don Miguel Ruiz, The Power of Now, by Eckert Tolle, The Highest Level of Enlightenment, by David Hawkins, Radical Self-Acceptance, by Tara Brach. 101 Ways To Transform Your Life, by Wayne Dyer.

Think of your mind as a lawn that needs daily watering.

Every day, read for one to twenty minutes, to gain more knowledge and freedom from new "sober" thoughts and ideas. Through Seasons of the Heart, John Powell, S.J., As Bill Sees It, by Bill Wilson, 365 TOA, by Den Ming-Dao, Words To Live By, by Easwaran, The Tao of Joy, by Derek Lin, 24 Hours A Day, by Hazelden Foundation, Touchstones, by Hazelden Foundation, Just For Today, by Narcotics Anonymous.

You can order all of these books and CD's on Amazon.com

ALTRUISM (Unselfish concern for the welfare of others.)

Become a giver rather than a taker. Faith, without works, is dead. It's a candle without a flame.

MYTH 8

THERE IS NO CURE FOR ADDICTION

"If one advances confidently in the direction of his dreams, and endeavors to live the life he has imagined, he will meet with a success unexpected in common hours." (Henry David Thoreau)

CLIFF PRENTISS, THE FOUNDER of *Cliffside Malibu*, a Five Star Luxury Rehab Facility in California, says he has found the cure for addiction. All the information can be found in his book, *The Alcoholism and Addiction Cure: A Holistic Approach to Total Recovery*.

Jack Trimpey, the founder of *Rational Recovery*, says he also has found a cure. You'll find all the details in his book, *Rational Recovery: The New Cure For Substance Addiction*.

Here's how the dictionary defines "cure."
1. A means of healing or restoring to health.
2. A means of correcting or relieving anything that is troublesome or detrimental.
3. To relieve or get rid of something detrimental, as an illness or a bad habit.

Based on that definition, there's another book you may want to read also, *Alcoholics Anonymous*. The original members of A.A. were "cured" in that they were able to get rid of a bad habit that was very detrimental to their health.

Sounds simple enough, but instead of reading all these books, what if... there was a pill you could take that would solve the problem. Well, there is, almost. It's the **Intervention Pill**, otherwise known as the "I" pill. If you are experiencing physical cravings, obsessive thoughts, or compulsive feelings, and you want to drink or use drugs to make those thoughts or feelings go away, all you have to do is take the **"I"** pill. Within five minutes, all thoughts about drinking or using drugs will vanish from your mind. You can be driving to the liquor store, pain clinic, or your drug dealer, and you'll turn around and go home - guaranteed.

The **"I"** pill is called **Super Ex-lax**. It will remind you that once you mix the "chemicals" in Ex-Lax, drugs, or alcohol with the "chemicals" in your body, the "chemicals" will then write the next chapter in the story of your life. While this pill doesn't actually exist, you can write *Post It Notes* in various places, with a big "S" on them. Tell everyone else that you have become religious, and it's there to remind you to *Seek*, so you can *Find*, or you can tell them that Superman is your hero. Only you have to know the truth. But, let's not forget what we suffer from, alcohol**ism**. No pill will ever take the **ism** away.

Someone once asked me what it was like being an alcoholic and drug addict. I said, "It's like being Captain of the Titanic, singing **My Way** as the ship is going down. I think this sums up our situation.

One of the primary reasons we think we can *control* our drinking or drug use is due to the months and years we had our brains bashed by the "chemicals" in pills, alcohol, and drugs.

Imagine, at the time of your birth, that the number of brain cells you started out with was equivalent to starting your life with a "full deck" of cards.

As we snort cocaine, swallow pills or alcohol, or shoot up with heroin, the "chemicals" in those drugs begin killing millions of brain cells. By the time we arrive at our first meeting, we are no longer playing with a "full deck" of cards. First to go are the Aces, followed by the Kings, Queens, and Jacks. When we lose access to the most powerful cards in our deck, it's no small wonder that so many of us think we can "control" our use of pills, alcohol, or drugs. We find ourselves in the mindset of Bill Wilson and every other "real" Alcoholic and drug addict.

"I began to waken very early in the morning shaking violently. A tumbler full of gin, followed by half a dozen bottles of beer would be required if I were to eat any breakfast. Nevertheless, I still thought I could control it." *(A.A. Page 5)*

This story has many variations.

I have a friend who cannot accept the fact that he is an alcoholic, even though he has been to treatment three times, has had three DUI's, has lost the right to drive for ten years, and recently spent 90 days in a local county jail.

Within days of getting out, he got drunk.

He still thinks he can **control** it. Why?

It's not because he is in denial.

You need a large number of healthy brain cells to deny something.

It's due to brain damage, his **inability** to *effectively* reason with himself and implement a decision for his own well being.

We Also Have The Story Of The "Real" Alcoholic

Many people assume that the only drug used by the original members of A.A. was alcohol.

Not true!

"If he can afford it, he may have liquor concealed all over his house, to be certain no one gets his entire supply away from him. As matters grow worse, he begins to use a combination of high powered sedatives and liquor to quiet his nerves, so he can go to work." *(A.A. Page 22)*

Both Bill Wilson and Dr. Bob, the co-founders of A.A., both accurately fit the description of the "real" alcoholic. *(A.A. Page 6, 176)*

FELLOWSHIP

Fellowship is one of the major benefits of being a member of a Twelve Step program. There are people in A.A. who are not "real" alcoholics, but they love the **fellowship** it provides.

They fall into two classes:

MODERATE DRINKERS

Moderate drinkers have little or no trouble stopping drinking. *(A.A. Page 20)*

HARD DRINKERS

Getting a DUI, faced with divorce or medical problems hard drinkers can stop drinking. *(A.A. P 21)*

THE "REAL" ALCOHOLIC.

This is what separates "us" from "them."

"At some stage of his drinking career, he begins to lose all control of his liquor consumption once he starts to drink." *(A.A. P 21)*

Within the rooms of A.A., there are moderate and hard drinkers who love the "fellowship" our program provides.

They don't need a spiritual experience to stop drinking.

They don't have to work the steps.

They don't have to get a sponsor.

But we do. Bill Wilson summed it up this way:

"Unless each A.A. member follows, to the best of their ability, our suggested 12 Steps to recovery, they almost certainly sign their own death warrant." *(12 Steps and 12 Traditions, Page 174)*

There's a story about a Chinese war lord, who, after conquering and imprisoning the soldiers he captured in battle, was approached by some local, wealthy merchants who wanted to supply the prisoners with water, food, and bedding because:
 a. The water they were drinking had parasites in it.
 b. The food was so bad, some of the prisoners were starving to death, and
 c. There was no bedding, just a concrete floor.
Since it didn't cost him any money, the Warlord agreed.
Six months later, the prisoners were much healthier.

Then, late one evening, a local monk, who had been given the key to the cells by a guard, snuck his way into the prison and opened up all the cell doors.

When the Warlord walked through the prison the next morning, only two of the cells were empty.

The remaining prisoners, comfortable in their new surroundings, decided to stay in prison.

This may explain why we choose the slavery of addiction over freedom of recovery.

Freedom doesn't come without a price.

The poem, PARROTMAN, provides some additional insights into why "we keep coming back" to what is comfortable and familiar in our lives.

PARROTMAN

The parrot proudly perched
On the branch outside her cage
As she sang her song of freedom
As she danced upon her stage.

And all who passed did marvel
At the sounds she did expel,
At the beauty of her pageantry
And the story she did tell.

But when she finished singing
Her keeper hooked her chain
Her face soon filled with sorrow
Her eyes soon filled with shame.

And I couldn't help but wonder
I couldn't help but guess
At why she didn't fly away
Why she settled for less.

But then I saw a mirror
Reflections of my past
The treatment centers I'd walked into
The recoveries that didn't last.

T'was then that I remembered
T'was then that I recalled
The boundaries of a cage
Are more secure than freedom's call.

TWELVE ANTIDOTES FOR ADDICTION

COURAGE
The quality of mind or spirit that enables a person to face difficulty or pain without fear, bravery.

COMMITMENT
To pledge, bind, or obligate oneself to achieve a goal; to burn the bridges of escape behind you.

HONESTY
Freedom from deceit or fraud, truthfulness, sincerity, or frankness.

HUMILITY
Free from vanity, boastfulness, or grandiosity; not arrogant, a realistic view of one's limitations.

DISCIPLINE
An exercise, regimen, or series of steps that improves one's skill and control.

FORTITUDE
Strength of mind that enables one to endure temporary pain or adversity with courage.

PERSISTENCE
To persevere in spite of difficulty, discomfort, discouragement, or obstacles.

FORGIVENESS
The wisdom and courage to let go of anger or resentment toward oneself, or another; compassion.

PATIENCE
Quietly and steadily persevering, bearing hardship, or discomfort with fortitude and calmness.

ALTRUISM
Unselfish concern for the welfare of others.

RESILIENCE
Springing back, rebounding; recovering from adversity.

TEAMWORK
Cooperative and coordinated effort with others to achieve a common goal.

It's said that "Meeting makers make it." Recovery isn't something we **make**. It's something we **do**. It's a daily radical choice; it's a journey, not a destination.

THE TWELVE STEPS OF RADICAL RECOVERY

HONESTY
We admitted that, "It's not a fair fight," that once we mix the **chemicals** in pills, alcohol or drugs with the chemicals in our body, the volcano of cravings erupt. Our brains get hijacked. We lose all access to rational thought, the love we have for our families, and our spiritual beliefs and moral values.

COURAGE
We were willing to stop wallowing in self-pity, and leave the comfort of that dark, dreary, and solitary prison we call addiction, and become open to the possibility that what lies behind us, and what lies before us, are tiny matters compared to what lies within us; that we are power-full.

SPIRITUALITY

We were willing to go to any lengths to wake up, feed, and nurture the *Sleeping Giant* inside us, so we could accomplish those things which we had never been able to accomplish on our own.

ENDURANCE

We were willing to endure the temporary pain and discomfort we felt as frozen feelings began to thaw, and we took an inventory of our lives.

CHANGE

We were willing to cast aside ideas, emotions, and attitudes, which were once the guiding forces of our lives, and make radical changes in the way we thought and felt by instilling – infusing slowly and gradually into our minds and hearts - the knowledge, wisdom, and experience of others.

COMMITMENT

We were willing to go to any lengths to achieve victory over our addiction to pills, alcohol, or drugs by using the Five Star Program of Radical Recovery as a barometer for measuring our progress each day: Read, exercise, make healthy food choices, meditate, and help another alcoholic or addict.

DESIRE

We were willing to transform our cravings for pills, alcohol and drugs into a burning desire for freedom from the slavery of addiction.

BELIEF

We came to believe that we could recover, mentally, emotionally, spiritually, and physically, and this belief fueled our enthusiasm and passion to recreate our lives by practicing a holistic lifestyle.

TEAMWORK

We were willing to become part of a team that provided us with the encouragement and support we needed to function at the highest level we were capable of performing: mentally, emotionally, spiritually, and physically.

FORTITUDE

We were willing to get anchored in our recovery and develop the resources that would enable us to endure and overcome the challenges we all face in life, to transform our stumbling stones into building blocks.

DISCIPLINE

We got real. Just as we had to spend time, energy, and money in developing the bad habits that enabled us to become alcoholics and addicts, we had an "epiphany," a sudden, intuitive perception and insight. We had to invest time, energy, and money in developing new, positive habits that would enable us to become addiction survivors.

ALTRUISM

We were willing to stop creating suffering in our lives and the lives of those we love, and then spend the rest of our lives doing something to help alleviate the suffering of others.

MYTH 9

WE HAVE TO GET OUT OF THE DRIVER'S SEAT

"Change and growth take place when a person has risked himself and dares to become involved with experimenting with his own life."(Herbert Otto)

THE DRIVER'S SEAT

TELLING NEWCOMERS THAT THEY HAVE to get "out" of the driver's seat makes a very false assumption, that they are "in" the driver's seat. The fact is, we stopped being "in" the driver's seat the day we became addicted to pills, alcohol, or drugs, and our brain got hijacked.

To begin our recovery journey, we have to get in the driver's seat by first taking responsibility for our recovery, then seeking guidance and direction, asking for help, and learning how to tame the obsessive thoughts, compulsive feelings, and physical cravings that create so much pain and suffering in our lives, and those we love.

How can we tame these powerful forces? Bill Wilson defined addiction as, "A cancer of the emotions and the soul." If you think of the "cancer" as an energy, a force, we have two choices:

1. Harness, guide, and direct this powerful force so that we can transform our cravings for pills, alcohol, or drugs into cravings for honesty, integrity, peace, and humility.
2. Let it continue to control and dominate our lives until it destroys us.

If we want to become addiction survivors, to become free from the slavery of addiction, then we have to STOP talking about or avoiding, what we think is the problem - alcohol and drugs. We have to invest time, energy, and money into healing the cancer of the emotions and the soul that is destroying our lives, so we can experience the personality change that is *required* to achieve permanent sobriety.

"Anyone who knows the alcoholic personality by first hand contact knows that no true alky ever stops drinking permanently without undergoing a profound personality change."*(As Bill Sees It - Page 1)*

Einstein said it this way:

"You can't solve a problem with the same mind that created it."

How much time, energy, and money did you *spend* on cigarettes, alcohol, or drugs over the past twelve months?

How much time, energy, and money are you willing to *invest* in your recovery so you can develop a healthy body, mind, emotions, and spirit?

Why is it important to do this? Because when we begin our recovery journey, we are like Humpty Dumpty.

**Humpty Dumpty sat on a wall.
Humpty Dumpty had a great fall.
All the King's horses and all the King's men, couldn't put Humpty Dumpty back together again.**

There's a story here. It's my story.
Maybe, it's your story too.

Imagine Humpty Dumpty showing up at a meeting and sharing his story. It might go something like this: Have you ever asked yourself "why" I was sitting on the wall?

Did I really fall, or did I jump? Was I "broken" before I actually hit the ground? Why couldn't all the King's horses and all the King's men put me back together again? I'll start my story by answering the last question first.

For me, all the King's horses, and all the King's men were the doctors, spouses, psychologists, ministers, employers, friends, relatives, and children who tried to *fix* me, but couldn't.

It wasn't their fault.

How could they, when, in spite of overwhelming evidence to the contrary, I refused to admit that I was broken.

WAS I "BROKEN" BEFORE I HIT THE GROUND?

Yes! Long before! And the worst part of my story is that I was *broken* by my three best friends. When I first met my friends, I was shy and insecure. All that disappeared the day we met. All the good things started to come my way: money, respect, and applause. And it was good, for a while, but there never seemed to be enough. I always wanted... more... doubles, or triples, of everything.

Then one day, my friends suddenly turned on me. My fears and insecurities came back - with a vengeance. I could manage the days. But the nights! Oh, how I hated the nights. I wanted to leave, but I couldn't. I had lost the ability to function without my friends being by my side. I was broken. No self-esteem! No self-worth! No self-love!

I stopped believing in myself, other people, and God. I felt angry, cheated, and was filled with self-hatred. I thought I was crazy. I felt like I was locked inside a cylinder. I couldn't get out, and no one else could get in.

When I drove past an airport, I would think about getting on a plane and just disappearing. I even thought about checking into the psychiatric ward of the local hospital, on one condition:

Once they locked me up, I wanted them to throw the key away. I no longer wanted to deal with reality. I hate to admit this, but there were many nights when I went to bed, and prayed... that I wouldn't wake up in the morning.

WHAT WENT WRONG?

I would like to tell you that my three friends were to blame; that it was their fault, then I wouldn't have to take responsibility for my fall. But, I can't.

In looking back, I can now see that what started out as a great and wonderful relationship, turned into a nightmare.

The nightmare started when I began to abuse my friends, and the more I abused my friends, the more my friends abused me. You see, my three friends were *Pills, Alcohol, and Drugs.* This brings us back to the beginning of the story. There I was, sitting on the wall.

DID I JUMP, OR DID I FALL?

I thought about jumping, many times, but I didn't.

While sitting on that wall of hopelessness and despair I reached deep inside myself, and summoned the courage to do something, something I had never done before.

I asked a friend for help; a friend who understood what I was experiencing because he had experienced it himself.

Here's what my friend told me.

I could use my fall as an *excuse* to play the role of a victim, which I felt very comfortable with, or I could use it to propel myself to a higher level of existence. If I chose to propel myself to a higher level of existence, he said I wouldn't have to do it alone. He, and a group of friends in recovery, would be with me - every step of the way, and after completing the Twelve Steps of recovery, he *guaranteed* me that I would know a new happiness, and a new freedom; that I would *experience* the peace I had been so desperately yearning for:

Peace... in the storms of life.

Peace... when I couldn't get my way.

Peace... when I couldn't be *Master of the Universe*, and rescue people from their pain and suffering.

Peace... with the human condition, with the *Humpty Dumpty* who hides behind all our masks.

I didn't believe him, but I had nothing to lose; *anything* was better than what I had. So, I swallowed what pride I had left, and followed his suggestions. To my surprise, he was right.

The peace and happiness I had sought in pills, alcohol, and drugs I found *within* myself. I didn't have to swallow, snort, inhale, or inject anything to experience this peace.

I just had to be willing to let go... of all my illusions about *who* and *what* I thought I was, let go of all the *labels* and *limitations* I had put on myself and that others had put on me.

Looking back, I now know that I was suffering from a case of *Terminal Uniqueness*.

I felt *completely isolated*, cut off, from everyone around me. As time passed, I found out that I wasn't alone in my isolation. I was just like *60 million other Americans* who consistently abuse pills, drugs, or alcohol.

I learned something else from my new friends. Pills, drugs, and alcohol were my *secondary addiction*.

My *primary* addiction was *escaping* from physical, mental, emotional, and spiritual pain. The pills, drugs, alcohol, sex, food, and gambling were simply the *fuels* I used to *escape* from my pain by creating a mood altering experience. I also learned that I had something in common with *every* human being on the planet. We all have the same characters in our story: The Good, The Bad, The Beautiful, and The Ugly. There are no *exceptions*.

We've all done things we consider bad or ugly.

What makes us *different* from each other, are the choices we make, *after* we get broken by our falls.

We can continue *numbing* the pain, or we can find the *courage* to create more good and beautiful in our lives.

Before starting the Twelve Steps of recovery, I had no coping skills. When I experienced physical, mental, emotional, or spiritual pain, I only had one choice.

I wanted to numb the pain... as quickly as possible.

Now, I can work my way through *any* pain I experience, with a little help from my friends, and the *Spirit* which lies deep inside us.

I grow stronger every time I make this choice.

It takes an *act of courage* to ask for help.

In the rooms of Alcoholics Anonymous and Narcotics Anonymous, there are tremendous resources and people, people who are willing to help *anyone* who wants to take responsibility for recreating their lives.

The first meeting I attended was an A.A. meeting. There, I was offered something I had wanted my whole life, *Unconditional love*.

I was blind to the unconditional love my family had given me. At first, I found it difficult to *accept* or *give* love.

I didn't trust... myself, or anyone else, including God, but they assured me that would change; that, as I *progressed* in my recovery, I would learn, perhaps for the first time, what it meant to *give* and *receive* love... unconditionally.

In the past, when someone mentioned the word *love,* I was drawn to it as a moth is drawn to a flame. But my interest was *always* focused on being on the *receiving* end of love; not the *giving* end of it.

Then someone gave me a copy of Luis Evely's poem, *Unconditional Love*. It helped me see that I had things backwards. I learned that if I wanted to *have* friends, I first had to *be* one. I also learned that addiction is a disease, but it's different from other diseases like cancer, or diabetes. *It's a spiritual disease*; one that fills alcoholics and addicts with the *venom* of loneliness, isolation, and despair. To help me understand this, my friend asked me a question. "Did you ever have a toothache?" "Yes," I replied.

"*Who* was your attention focused on, when your mouth was throbbing with pain?" I said, "Myself."

"*What* was all your attention focused on, when your mouth was throbbing with pain?"

"The pain," I said.

I understood what he was trying to tell me. My addiction to pills, alcohol, and drugs was like a toothache. But it was a throbbing *spiritual pain* which made death look attractive, and made me *incapable* of loving anyone - because all my time and resources were spent thinking about, obtaining, using, or recovering from my substance use.

UNCONDITIONAL LOVE
Luis Evely

Loving people means summoning them forth with the loudest and most insistent of calls. It means stirring up in them a mute and hidden being who can't help leaping at the sound of our voice. A being so new that even those who carried him didn't know him, and yet so authentic that they can't fail to recognize him once they discover him.

All love includes fatherhood and motherhood. To love, is to bid someone to live, to invite them to grow. Since people don't have the courage to mature unless someone has faith in them, we have to reach those we meet at the level where they stopped developing, where they were given up as hopeless and so withdrew into themselves and began to secrete a protective shell because they thought they were alone and no one cared.

They have to feel they are loved very deeply and very boldly before they are willing to remove that protective shell, and appear humble, kind, affectionate, and vulnerable.

WHAT IF...

You have a purpose, a mission, a very specific reason for being on this planet, like Oskar Schindler, the selfish, self-centered, egotistical, greedy, arrogant, lustful businessman, who, in World War 2, experienced what can only be called a *spiritual awakening*.

He experienced this when he saved the lives of six hundred Polish Jews, and gave life to the generations which followed. He did this by spending every penny he had bribing Nazi officers, to keep them from sending Jews to death camps.

WHAT IF...

All the guilt and shame you have about your addiction, and the things you did, while you were active in your addiction was your *training ground* for experiencing a *spiritual awakening*, a journey from darkness to light.

It is during this journey that your guilt and shame gets *transformed* into great compassion and love for people just like yourself. The people who can't get off the *Relapse Roller Coaster Ride*, the people who hide behind walls of deafening silence, where they are *emotionally Invisible* to those they love.

The people who think they are alone, and no one cares. The people who need to feel they are loved very deeply and very boldly, before they are willing to take down their walls, and appear humble, kind, affectionate, sincere, and vulnerable.

WHAT IF...

Your purpose, your mission, is to become an Oskar Schindler, someone who can save lives, and impact future generations to come, by helping other addicts and alcoholics escape from the slavery of addiction.

But what if... you never showed up to open the door of the cage for them, because you bought into the idea that you are a *victim*, that you are *powerless* over your addiction. So, you never took the *Twelve Simple Steps* to awaken the *Power* of the *Sleeping Giant* deep inside you, The *Power* that transforms cravings for pills, drugs, and alcohol into cravings for freedom, honesty, integrity, humility, and peace.

We love heroes, someone who can take on, or overcome great obstacles. Someone who gives us the courage to believe in ourselves.

In recovery, the Twelve Steps, the *process* is the hero. But why don't we put a name and face on our hero. He's Humpty Dumpty!

You can put him on your key ring, coffee cup, t-shirt, or dashboard of your car.

The next time you feel like *escaping* from some physical, mental, emotional, or spiritual pain, he will be there:

To support you...
To encourage you...

- Kelly -

To remind you that...
What all the King's horses, and all the King's men couldn't do, we can do - together.

MYTH 10

THE STEPS SHOULD BE TAKEN IN ORDER

"We are what we repeatedly do. Excellence, then, is not an act but a habit. Habits start out as cobwebs and then become cables." (John J. Murphy)

IF THE STEPS SHOULD BE taken in order, then logic dictates that no one should take a daily inventory, pray, meditate, or help another alcoholic or drug addict until they have completed the first Nine Steps.

Steps 10, 11, and 12 are Maintenance Steps.

They can be started the first day we stop drinking or using drugs.

It's the first Nine Steps that should be taken in order.

Maybe one of the reasons A.A. had a much higher recovery rate than what we are experiencing today is newcomers, working with more experienced members of A.A., were encouraged to help those less fortunate than themselves.

This was probably based on Bill Wilson's personal experience.

During the first six months of his recovery he worked with many alcoholics, but he was the only one who stayed sober.

Where did this idea come from, that all Twelve Steps should be taken in order?

Perhaps we can find the answer in A.A.'s deeper roots.

Before A.A. got started in 1935, if the local town drunk or drug addict wanted to stop popping pills, drinking alcohol, or using drugs they often turned to the *Temperance Society*.

The dictionary defines these terms as follows:

Temperance: Total abstinence from alcohol, and any other mood altering substance, or behavior.

Society: An organized group of people joined together for a common purpose.

How did the members of the *Temperance Society* get clean and sober?

They just didn't pick up a drink or drug.

How did the original members of the *Temperance Society* stay clean and sober?

They just didn't pick up, and went to a lot of meetings.

Perhaps this is the origin of the slogan:

"Meeting makers make it."

The common purpose of the members of the Temperance Society was to encourage each other to abstain from using pills, alcohol, or drugs, one day at a time, and regularly attend meetings.

While the group had a *common purpose,* the focus of each member was always "intensely personal," avoid the intense pain and suffering they always experienced after they drank, or used drugs.

Maybe this is where we got the slogan:

"Just don't pick up, no matter what!"

At their meetings, the members would tell war stories about what happened when they drank, or used drugs, and how they ended up in jail, or lost their minds, jobs, families, self-respect, etc.

The *Temperance Society* was the first *Twelve Step Program* in America.

What steps did they take to get clean and sober?

THE TWELVE STEPS OF THE TEMPERANCE SOCIETY

Here are the steps they took to stop drinking and using drugs:

1. We admitted we were powerless over alcohol and drugs, because when we drank or used drugs, we thought and did crazy and insane things.
2. We came to believe that our "common purpose," abstaining from taking pills, drinking, or using drugs, one day at a time, would enable us to do together, what we had not been able to do by ourselves.
3. We became teachable. The lesson we learned was simple. *People who attended meetings got clean and sober. People who didn't attend meetings got drunk or high.* So, we made meeting power our God, because without meetings, we had no power; and without power, we had no hope.
4. We did things we were ashamed of when we drank or used drugs. But once we stopped, most of us returned to being the saints we were *before* we became alcoholics and addicts. So, there was no need to do any kind of moral inventory. We knew that pills, alcohol, and drugs were our problem and abstinence was the solution. And saints don't need to do moral inventories.
5. We admitted to ourselves that we needed to change. So, instead of using pills, alcohol, or drugs, we started to smoke more cigarettes and drink more coffee. When

- Radical Recovery -

that desire to *escape from reality* reared its ugly head, we were able to replace the craving for pills, alcohol, or drugs with a craving for nicotine, food, shopping, sex, porno, 15 hour work days, or the rush that comes with gambling. We claim progress; not perfection.

6. After completing the first five steps, we were entirely ready to sign a pledge that we would use the willpower and *self-knowledge* we acquired to *never* pick up a another pill, drink, or drug.
7. Having been fully restored to our original state of righteousness, the defects of others started to stand out like sore thumbs, and we let them know it.
8. We made a list of triggers, the people, places, and things that could cause us to relapse, and vowed revenge on anyone that pushed the buttons that made us pick up a pill, drink, or drug.
9. Every human being makes mistakes, so we purchased a helium balloon, wrote the word PAST on it, and let it go, far, far, far away.
10. As we grew in wisdom, we took the focus off ourselves and began focusing on those less fortunate than ourselves. We realized that there were many people who were not as righteous as we were; that included our parents, spouses, children, relatives, and co-workers. We began to tell them what they needed to do to "straighten up and fly right," and when we were right, we promptly admitted it.
11. Most of us believed in some God, so as we grew spiritually, we began to pray to Him, asking that He reveal the special mission He had for us. Was it to bring peace to the Jews and Arabs? Perhaps straighten out the Protestants and Catholics in Northern Ireland? We were ready to get on the white horse, which we knew He would provide, when the time was right.
12. Getting a wake-up call as a result of these steps, we attended newcomer meetings to keep our fears green. When newcomers relapsed *we thanked them for taking those pills, drinks, or drugs for us,* wished them good

luck, and told them to keep coming back until they got "IT."

By now, you have probably figured out that the *Twelve Steps of the Temperance Society* are a figment of my imagination, or are they?

Has A.A. and N.A. become a *Temperance Society* where the "common purpose" is to abstain from using pills, drugs, or alcohol *one day at a time*, and regularly attend meetings?

If the *Temperance Society* actually existed today, would it be identical to A.A. or N.A?

For some of us, whose sole purpose is to *avoid picking up a pill, drink, or drug one day at a time*, the answer would be "Yes!"

But the *primary focus* of A.A. and N.A. is based on *connecting with others* who have an addiction to pills, drugs, or alcohol.

The irony is, that, by getting all the attention off ourselves and helping others, we feel better about ourselves.

Because we're helping others, our self-esteem increases; when that happens, we increase the odds of staying clean and sober, dramatically.

At the beginning of our recovery journey, many of us find ourselves in the position of the person described in the poem, THE MUTE.

THE MUTE

How many are we whose muted feelings
drive us
to seek the safety of solitary prisons
where imaginary lovers comfort us
with illusions of intimacy?

How many are we whose secrets
buried alive
continue to smolder
like the embers of a raging forest fire
that's run its course?

How many are we whose amnesia
protects us
from memories
too painful to recall?

How many are we whose hostage hearts
yearn
for patient hands,
trusting eyes
and
gentle voices
that will give us the courage
to emerge from isolation?

How many are we
whose freedom can only be found
in giving
what we need to get?
Here's the *simple approach* that worked for the original A.A. members:

"If an alcoholic fails to perfect and enlarge their spiritual life through work and self-sacrifice for others, they cannot survive the certain trials and low spots ahead." *(A.A. Page 15)*

This brings us to the question of "powerlessness." Recognizing that our love affair with pills, alcohol, or drugs has become an *abusive relationship*, and that the battle we're fighting with the **chemicals** in pills, alcohol, and drugs is one *we can't win*, brings us to that *epiphany*, that sudden and intuitive perception of reality. *It's not a fair fight.*

It's a rematch of David and Goliath, but David can't win this battle unless he learns new coping skills.

WHAT ABOUT THE LOVE WE HAVE FOR OUR PARENTS, SPOUSE, PARTNER, OR CHILDREN?

Once the *cravings* kick in, the love disappears, like the beautiful woman behind the magician's cape.

WHAT ABOUT THE KNOWLEDGE WE ACQUIRED FROM MEETINGS AND TREATMENT CENTERS?

It turns to mush when the waves of obsessive thoughts, compulsive feelings, and physical cravings kick in.

The problem we face is this:

We have lost the power to control the *obsessive thoughts, compulsive feelings, and physical cravings* which have such an insatiable appetite.

That's the bad news.

But here's the good news.

While we may have lost control, we can get it back, in spades.

Are you ready to admit that once you mix the *chemicals* in pills, alcohol, or drugs with the *chemicals* in your body, using your *willpower* to stop the cravings becomes as useless as using your willpower to try and stop the Nor'easter that hit New York and New Jersey in 2012.

If you answered "Yes," congratulations, you just jumped your **first hurdle** on the road to becoming an addiction survivor.

Are you ready to admit that you get an "F" for *effectively* managing your obsessive thoughts, compulsive feelings, and physical cravings?

If you answered "Yes," then, congratulations, you just jumped your **second hurdle** on the road to becoming an "addiction survivor."

The next hurdle is a lot higher than the last two you just jumped. It has two parts.

Do you believe that you are more than what you see when you look in the mirror, more than a combination of obsessive thoughts, compulsive feelings, and physical cravings?

Are you open to the possibility that you just might have access to a Power, deep inside you, that can provide you with the courage and commitment you need to tame your thoughts, feelings, and cravings, so they can better serve you, rather than control and dominate you?

If you answered "Yes," congratulations!

You just jumped over your **third hurdle** on the road to becoming an addiction survivor.

The **fourth hurdle**.

This is the biggest one, so far.

Are you willing to make a decision to do "whatever it takes" to access this Power inside you, and pray, real hard, for the courage to do the work that is guaranteed to provide you with the resources you need to free yourself from the slavery of addiction?

If you answered "Yes," congratulations!

You just jumped your **fourth hurdle** on the road to becoming an "addiction survivor."

Why is it important to jump these hurdles?

Because, as mentioned repeatedly, addiction isn't a disease. Left untreated, it is a terminal disease.

What's the treatment?

Just as chemo-therapy has been proven to be an effective method for treating cancer, the Twelve Steps have been proven to be an effective method for treating *The Disease of Chemical Dependency.*

- *Kelly* -

It has been said that the answers we are looking for, how to free ourselves from *The Slavery of Addiction*, and live serene, useful, and productive lives, can be found in the book *Alcoholics Anonymous*.

But simply knowing *where* the answers are, isn't enough.

We have to know *what* questions to ask. The quality of our questions, will determine the quality of our sobriety.

Before using the following questions as a barometer to check your *motives* and your *ability*, as a human being, to rationalize behavior that's going to end up hurting you, or someone else, it is important that you decide which type of sobriety you want to achieve, just physical sobriety, or physical and emotional sobriety.

QUALITY QUESTIONS

1. Will this choice increase my self-esteem, or will it make me feel guilty and ashamed?
2. Will this choice make me part of the solution, or part of the problem?
3. Am I seeking truth, or am I seeking a way to rationalize negative or self-destructive behavior?
4. Am I choosing to be self-righteous and resentful, or compassionate and forgiving?
5. The purpose of the Twelve Steps is to help us *conform* our will to God's Will. Is the action I am about to take in accordance with God's Will: Love, trust, forgiveness, compassion, and gratitude, or my will: Jealousy, fear, resentment, self-righteousness, and self-pity?
6. Does this situation require *faith* or does it really require the *courage* to take action?
7. Will this choice give me more *freedom*, or will it make me a *slave* to the cravings, obsessions, and compulsions of the past?
8. Will this choice bring me long term happiness and fulfillment, or short term gratification that will end in suffering?
9. Am I honestly expressing my thoughts and feelings, or am I trying to please someone else because I believe *being liked* by them is more important than *being honest* with them?

10. Am I being grateful for all I have, or ungrateful for not getting something I want?
11. Will I use this situation as an opportunity to learn from my mistakes, like other human beings, or will I use it to beat myself up, again, for not being perfect?
12. Am I about to love and nurture myself, or sabotage my success?

MYTH 11

OUR DISEASE SPEAKS TO US

"It takes more courage to reveal insecurities than to hide them, more strength to relate to people than to dominate them, more manhood to abide by thought-out principles rather than blind reflex. Toughness is in the soul and spirit, not in muscles and an immature mind " (Alex Karras)

Let's assume you smoked two packs of cigarettes a day for twenty years, and you decided to stop smoking.

You've managed to put together 21 days without picking up a cigarette.

You arrive at work and your boss hands you a pink slip. She tells you the company needs to lay off one hundred people, and you're one of them.

When you got bad news in the past, the first thing you always did was reach for a cigarette.

So, what's the first thing you do?

You reach for a cigarette.

Would you say that this reaction on your part was a **disease** that was "speaking" to you, or would you say it was an *unhealthy coping skill* that had become a deeply ingrained **habit**?

Let's assume you're an alcoholic or drug addict.

You're in your third week of recovery.

You arrive at work and your boss hands you a pink slip. She tells you the company needs to lay off one hundred people, and you're one of them.

When you got bad news in the past, the first thing you always did was reach for a pill, drink, or a drug.

So, what's the first thing you do?

You reach for a pill, drink, or a drug!

Would you say that this reaction on your part was a **disease** that was speaking to you, or would you say it was an *unhealthy coping skill* that had become a deeply ingrained **habit**?

We have to reach out for a pill, drink, or drug. They don't reach out for us. Nor, to the best of my knowledge, does the disease of *Chemical Dependency* have the ability to "speak."

Then, what is it that "speaks" to us?

Our **dis-ease** "speaks" to us; not our disease.

Our **dis-ease** is created by *feelings* such as fear, anger, anxiety, resentment, self-pity, depression, guilt, shame, boredom, and despair.

Feelings are not a disease.

They are emotional reactions to the way we think about events that happen in our lives.

It's **A, B, C, D.**

A. Event: Getting laid off.
B. Thought: "I won't be able to pay the rent."
C. Feeling: Fear
D. Habit: "If I take a drink, snort cocaine, pop a pill, or smoke some weed, I can make the *feeling* go away."

On the other hand, if you have been diagnosed as being paranoid schizophrenic, you definitely have a disease that "speaks" to you.

We are not in the same boat as schizophrenics.

We are in the same boat as everyone else on the planet. The root of all our problems come from the same three sources: Delusional Thinking, Destructive Emotions, and Physical Cravings.

Distressing feelings such as anger, resentment, guilt, shame and boredom are not diseases that make us want to pick up a pill, drink, or drug. They come under the heading of *destructive emotions.*

To prevent a relapse, it's important to make a distinction between our disease and our **dis-ease**.

Our disease has a name, *Chemical Dependency.*

It has four major characteristics.
1. It is chronic.
2. It is predictable.
3. It is progressive, and
4. It is fatal - if left untreated.

CHRONIC

What does chronic mean?

It's like diabetes, in that once we have it, it's not going to go away. It means we will never be able to *safely* use pills, alcohol, or drugs.

What makes us different from people who can *safely* drink a glass of wine or take a narcotic prescription drug?

When we mix the chemicals in alcohol or drugs with the chemicals in our bodies, it's no different than mixing the chemicals in Ex-lax with the chemicals in our bodies. In both cases, we become *powerless.* The chemical then writes the next chapter in the story of our lives; not our rational thoughts, not the loving feelings we have for our families, not our spiritual beliefs or moral values.

Our Disease Is Predictable, Progressive, and Fatal

What does this mean?
1. It means that addiction, left untreated, is a terminal disease. We die from it.
2. It means we go through three very predictable stages where our mental, emotional, spiritual, and physical health gets progressively worse.

Occasional Use

This is Stage One. This is where we begin our love affair with pills, drugs and alcohol. We feel wonderful together. A great couple.

Frequent Use

This is Stage Two.
We start making demands.
We need "more" to get the same good feelings. Our relationship with our drug of choice begins to interfere with our other responsibilities. We become preoccupied with the thought of how and when we'll get together again. We start missing appointments. We show up late for work. We miss work. We are now in an abusive relationship.

Consistent Use

This is Stage Three. Our abusive relationship now becomes a love-hate relationship, a *master-slave relationship*. Our *Master* compels us to do things we thought we would never do.
We lie.
We cheat.
We steal time or money from those who love us.
We stop showing up for life.
We forget about our responsibilities.
We do anything the Master wants just to have a few moments of bliss together.
We can't live with our Master.
We can't live without our Master.
We are now *chemically dependent*.
We have lost the ability to feel good on our own.

The only time we feel good is when we have a pill, drink, or drug inside our bodies.

Which Stage are you at now?
___ Stage 1
___ Stage 2
___ Stage 3
___ I am done. I surrender.

HOW DO WE "TREAT" OUR DISEASE?

We have to become stronger than the cravings for pills, alcohol, or drugs, stronger that the obsessive thoughts and compulsive feelings that control our lives.

HOW DO WE BECOME STRONGER?

Buddha and Bill Wilson had some things in common. Both agreed that if we wanted to be happy, joyous, and free, two things had to happen.
1. We had to stop creating suffering in our lives, and the lives of those we love.
2. We had to spend the rest of our lives doing something to alleviate the suffering of other people.

How did Bill and Buddha stop creating suffering in their lives and the lives of those they loved? They **meditated,** every day.

Let's take a look at the role meditation played in the lives of the original members of A.A.

"We clean house with the family, asking each morning in meditation that our creator show us the way of patience, tolerance, kindliness and love." *(A.A. Page 83)*

If we focused more of our attention on **doing** something instead of trying to **avoid** doing something, like picking up a pill, drink, or drug, one day at a time, there is no doubt in my mind that we would have an enormous increase in the recovery rate.

Are we literally, killing newcomers with kindness, when we *water down the message* passed on to us by the 100 original members of A.A., and tell them that chairs, doorknobs, key chains, salt shakers, and toilet paper, powers *less than* themselves, can restore them to sanity?

Are we promoting a sense of hopelessness when we tell newcomers that they will *never* be relieved of their addiction to pills, alcohol, or drugs; that it's going to be a *lifetime* battle?

Have we become deaf to the message of hope we hear at every A.A. meetings?

"That no *human* power (or inanimate object) could relieve us of our alcoholism, but God could and would if He were sought." *(A.A. Page 60)*

Are we promoting a constant diet of pie and ice cream (Meeting Makers Make It), without introducing the meat and potatoes of the program:

"What we really have is a daily reprieve contingent on the maintenance of our spiritual condition."*(A.A. Page 85)*

Where did the original members of A.A. find the **Power** to transform their craving for alcohol and drugs into a craving for freedom and integrity?

"We found the *Great Reality* deep down inside us. In the last analysis, it is only there that He may be found. It was so with us." *(A.A. Page 55)*

The poem, SLEEPING GIANTS, gives us some insight into *how* we can find the *Great Reality* deep down inside us.

- Kelly -

SLEEPING GIANTS

Each seed I see
Comes wrapped in a cloak
Filled with pregnant potential;
Waiting to be awakened
By a gentle and loving Spirit
Whose potent power
Transforms hard shells to
Soft, fragrant flowers.

Each person I see
Comes wrapped in a cloak
Filled with pregnant potential;
Waiting to be awakened
By a gentle and loving Spirit
Whose potent power
Transforms base instincts to
Noble virtues.

Neither fame nor fortune
Can achieve such transformation
But only a soul
Willing to surrender
To the womb of silence
Within.

MYTH 12

WILL-POWER IS USELESS WITH ADDICTION

"Nothing in the world can take the place of persistence. Talent will not! Nothing is more common than unsuccessful men with talent. Genius will not! Unrewarded genius is almost a proverb. Education will not! The world is full of educated failures. Persistence and determination alone are omnipotent." (Calvin Coolidge)

ACCORDING TO BILL WILSON:
"No one ought to say the A.A. program requires no willpower; here (Step 5) is one place you may require all you've got." *(Twelve Steps and Twelve Traditions - Page 61)*

In order to understand the role that will-power plays in addiction, we have to make a distinction between *will* and *power*. We also have to make a distinction between *willful and willing*. Two other important ingredients in the equation for becoming an addiction survivor are *motivation* and *desire*.

WILL: The **power** of the mind to control our actions and reactions; the **power** of being able to choose how we act.

Our will can be strong or weak, but in addiction the will is neither. It doesn't exist because we have no power. We are *powerless* because we have lost our minds. We have lost the *power* to **control** our actions and reactions to mood altering substances. We have lost the *power* of being able to **choose** whether or not we will drink or use drugs.

A physician friend of mind related this story to me.

"I knew that continued use of drugs could ruin my career and destroy me and my family's future.

When I got the urge to use, I would take out the picture of my wife and baby and say:

'You won't do this to them.'

Sometimes I would stare at the picture for ten minutes, then shoot up."

Our birth right as human beings is freedom. We have the power to tame our cravings, obsessions, and compulsions. But every time we put a pill, drink, or drug inside our body we become less than human because we lose our freedom.

The chemicals in alcohol and drugs trigger something similar to a volcanic eruption when they reach our brain. They release a tsunami of cravings which cut off all access to rational thought, the love we have for our families, and our spiritual beliefs and moral values.

POWER: Strength, might, or force, a great ability to do or act; capable of doing or accomplishing something.

Willpower, the ability to control our impulses, actions, and reactions, begins to play a positive role in recovery when we add the ingredient of:

MOTIVATION: The process that arouses, sustains, and regulates our behavior.

In recovery, the First Step in activating the *process* that arouses, sustains, and regulates our behavior is admitting that once we mix the chemicals in pills, alcohol, or drugs with the chemicals in our bodies we become **powerless**. The next step in the process is admitting that our lives are unmanageable; that we **lack the power** to control the obsessive thoughts, compulsive feelings, and physical cravings that govern our lives.

The obstacle that stands in our way of getting motivated, of gaining access to a Power that can free us from the slavery of addiction is that fact that we are willful.

WILLFUL: Pigheaded, inflexible, reckless, self-willed. One who stubbornly insists upon doing as he or she pleases; especially in opposition to those whose wishes or advice ought to be respected.

Transforming our **willfulness** into **willingness** opens the door to the world of recovery.

WILLING: Ready, favorably disposed or inclined.

Willingness gives us the motivation we need to sustain and regulate our behavior, the motivation to follow directions: Get a sponsor to guide us through the Twelve Steps, read recovery literature, attend meetings, and practice the spiritual principles of the Twelve Steps in our daily lives.

The last ingredient needed to become an addiction survivor is desire.

DESIRE: A longing or craving for something that brings satisfaction or enjoyment.

Addiction, is an energy, a force. If we guide and direct this powerful force, it transforms our longing and cravings for pills, alcohol, and drugs into a longing and craving for freedom, honesty, integrity, humility and peace. It opens up a world of intuition, creativity, imagination, and power. If we don't guide and direct this force, it destroys us.

A letter by Bill Wilson, written in 1966 summarizes all these points.

"We A.A's know the futility of trying to break the drinking obsession by will power alone. However, we do know that it takes a great deal of willingness to adopt A.A.'s Twelve Steps as a way of life that can restore us to sanity." (As Bill Sees It - Page 88)

The freedom we can achieve through the Twelve Steps can best be illustrated by the following story.

One Saturday morning, a man went to the beach to get a suntan. After 30 minutes, he felt this shadow come over him. He opened his eyes and saw a 6'5"muscle bound guy standing over him. The next thing he knew, he was waking up in the emergency room of a hospital with tiny slits for eyes. The nurse standing over him asked, "What happened to you?"

He replied, "I was at the beach getting a sun tan when, for no reason, this crazy lunatic came along and beat the hell out of me."

"That's the Bully," said the nurse.

"You are the fourth person this month that he has beat up. If I were you, I would stay away from the beach. Whatever pleasure or enjoyment you may get from it, it is not worth the risk."

For six months, all went well. He stayed away from the beach. Then one Sunday morning he said to himself, "Maybe the Bully doesn't go to the beach on Sunday. I think I'll check it out."

So, he went to the beach, and as luck would have it, the Bully was not there. He spread out his blanket on the sand and all went well for a while. But then it happened, the shadow, the Bully, and the emergency room. The same nurse was there. She knew what happened. She said: "You went back to the beach, didn't you? Are you crazy? You need to stay away from the beach. There's a meeting here on Tuesday night for people who have been beat up by the Bully. They encourage and support each other to stay away from the beach. You should attend it."

The next Tuesday night, he went to the meeting. He heard story after story from the people there about how they had been beaten up by the *Bully*. But there was a man there who looked like Rambo. After the meeting, he walked up to him and asked, "Do you mind if I ask you why you are at this meeting?"

Rambo replied: "I am here to support and encourage you to stay away from the beach so you don't get beat up by the Bully."

"But you don't look like you would have a problem with the Bully," said the newcomer.

"I don't," said Rambo, "Would you like to have the freedom of being able to go to the beach without being beat up by the Bully?"

"You bet! I love the beach," said the newcomer.

"Then tomorrow morning, meet me at the gym at 5 AM, and every morning thereafter, for the next three years."

The newcomer replied: "5 AM! Every morning! Three years! Are you serious?"

"Very serious," Rambo replied.

"The freedom you want is not free. It has to be earned. You have to pay a price. Are you willing to pay the price, or do you just like to talk about freedom?"

And the newcomer did it, 5 AM, every morning, for three years, until he looked like Rambo.

Then he went to the beach.

As he was looking out at the ocean, the Bully walked by. They looked each other in the eye, and there was this "mutual respect" for the power each of them had. No battle, no fight.

Note that he didn't put himself in the presence of the Bully until *after* he developed the courage, power, and strength he needed to face him without fear.

Here's Bill Wilson' view on the freedom we gain access to *after* we complete the Twelve Steps.

"Assuming we are spiritually fit, we can do all sorts of things alcoholics are not supposed to do. " *(A.A. Page 100)*

This all sounds wonderful in theory, but practically speaking, how do we achieve this freedom?

There is an arch we can walk through, and once having walked through this arch we can let go of our fears of today, tomorrow, and the hereafter because the road we are walking on is built on a firm foundation.

Walking on this foundation enables us to sustain our freedom.

THE ARCH

"This is the how and why of it. First of all, we had to quit playing God. It didn't work. Next, we decided that hereafter in this drama of life, God was going to be our Director. He is the Principal; we are his agents. Most good ideas are simple, and this concept was the keystone of the new and triumphant arch through we passed to freedom." *(A.A. Page 62)*

A keystone is the wedge-shaped piece at the summit of an arch, regarded as holding the other pieces in place.

THE FOUNDATION

"Helping others is the foundation stone of your recovery. A kindly act once in a while isn't enough. You have to act the Good Samaritan every day, if need be." *(A.A. Page 97)*

A foundation stone represents the nominal starting place in the construction of a monumental building, something that is essential and indispensible, the chief foundation on which something is constructed.

If you were one of the original members of A.A., what help would you have been expected to offer newcomers?

"It may mean the loss of many nights' sleep, great interference with your pleasures, interruptions to your business." *(A.A. Page 97)*

Today, if these were the requirements for being a member of A.A. or N.A., and you were arrested for being a member of a Twelve Step program, would there be enough evidence to convict you?

For the most part, treatment centers now offer the help that was initially provided by the original members of A.A.

Then, what is our primary responsibility to the newcomer? According to Bill Wilson:

"Our primary responsibility to the newcomer is an adequate presentation of the Twelve Steps." *(As Bill Sees It, Page 105)*

Based on your understanding of the Twelve Steps, answer the following questions True or False

1. The primary reason people relapse is that they stop going to meetings. T F
2. The original members of A.A. were *"real alcoholics;"* and not addicted to pills, morphine, etc. T F
3. K.I.S.S. The message for the newcomer must be simple: "Just don't pick up and go to meetings." T F
4. The 12 Steps are *suggestions* we can choose to follow. There are no *requirements* in our recovery program. T F

- Kelly -

5. The main purpose of the *12 Steps* is to help us abstain from using alcohol or drugs *one day at a time*. T F
6. Almost without exception, alcoholics and addicts *cannot* recover on their own. Recovery depends on meetings. T F
7. Newcomers who have not completed *all* Twelve Steps should not being offering help to other newcomers. T F
8. When we become willing to turn our will and life over to the care of God, as each of us understands Him, we will then get clean and sober. T F
9. A newcomer should wait a *minimum* of 90 days before starting their fourth step. T F
10. To protect ourselves from relapsing, we should avoid any triggers that might cause a relapse. T F
11. Reality! Relapses occur. When this happens, one should then double the number of meetings they attend. T F
12. The main purpose for attending meetings is to keep the consequences of addiction green, so we don't forget. T F
13. Every alcoholic and addict should begin each day by asking God to help them not pick up a drink or drug for 24 hours. T F
14. Every alcoholic/addict should end each day by thanking God for keeping them clean and sober for 24 hours. T F
15. Some of us have taken hard knocks to learn this truth: *To stop drinking or using drugs we must attend meetings.* T F
16. To *get* and *stay* clean and sober, we must be willing to go to any length to avoid picking up a pill, drink or drug. T F
17. After reading the Big Book, newcomers must decide for themselves whether or not if they want to stop drinking. T F
18. Burn the idea into the consciousness of the newcomer that: "Meeting makers make it." T F
19. The Twelve Steps should be taken in order. Don't pray or meditate until you have completed the first ten Steps with your sponsor. T F

20. Just as God gave Moses the Ten Commandments, He gave Bill Wilson *The Twelve Steps*. T F
21. To avoid relapsing, we must accept the fact that our battle with pills, alcohol, or drugs will be a lifetime battle. T F

All the answers are FALSE.

This doesn't mean that there is no "truth" in these statements.

Telling newcomers to avoid people, places, and things is certainly good advice. But you won't find any of this "advice" in the books *Alcoholics Anonymous, Twelve Steps and Twelve Traditions*, or *As Bill Sees It*.

Instead of telling newcomers to focus their attention on *avoidance*, "Just don't pick up a pill, drink or drug," our recovery literature focuses the newcomer's attention on taking *action*.

For example, let's take number 13:

Every alcoholic/addict should begin each day by asking God to help them not to pick up for 24 hours.

"Ask Him in your morning meditation what you can do each day for the person who is still sick." *(A.A. Page 64)*

How does this compare with:

"God, I would like you to serve **Me** today. Keep **Me** from picking up a pill, drink, or drug so I don't end up in divorce court, detox, jail, or dead."

Why isn't there any reference to alcohol or drugs?

"Because the problem has been removed. It doesn't exist for us." *(A.A. P 85)*

"More and more we became interested in what we could contribute to life." *(A.A. Page 63)*

For the original members of A.A, after the problem had been removed, after the ideas, emotions, and attitudes which were once the guiding forces of their lives were cast to one side, a completely new set of conceptions and motives began to dominate them.

What were the completely new set of conceptions and motives that began to dominate them?

The answer to this question can be found in the promises. *(A.A. Page 83)*

SUMMARY

"The power to affect your future lies within your own hands. Reach farther, aim higher, go the distance." (Nido Qubein)

I HAVE SEEN MANY YOUNG men and women come to treatment three times - in the same year. For those who don't die along the way, the lifetime average is about seven times.

Why?

The answer should be obvious.

Brain damage!

It comes from the beating and battering their brains receive by the **chemicals** in pills, alcohol, and drugs.

They look - but they don't see

They hear - but they don't listen.

They touch - but they don't feel.

They read - but they don't comprehend.

Based on the tragic failure rate experienced by those of us afflicted with *The Disease of Chemical Dependency*, we have to wonder if much progress has been made since 1935 when:

"Among physicians, the general opinion seems to be that most chronic alcoholics are doomed." (A.A. P XXX)

Don't despair!

There's hope!

The truth, if we can accept it, will set us free.

Here's the truth.

"There is no overnight fix for recovery.

To establish a viable recovery process takes at least three and a half years and for most, up to five years.

Becoming sober is not the hardest part.

Staying sober is.

Making changes in our lives halts the pain.

Keeping the changes is what saves our lives." *(Recovery Zone, Volume 1, Patrick Carnes, Ph.D.)*

Wishing for change doesn't work.

Waiting for change doesn't work.

Praying for change doesn't work.

Faith doesn't work because faith, without works, is dead.

What works, is action; the willingness to do the work.

Like a large ship sailing across the ocean, an addictive lifestyle carries a great deal of momentum.

If the captain of a large ship wants to make a u turn, there is only one way to do it, slowly.

It requires patience and diligence.

The only way to become an addiction survivor is to have infinite patience with the process, to be diligent, to make a constant and earnest effort to stay on course as we encounter the challenges of everyday life.

Also, many of us are often haunted by past mistakes, by the amount of time we spent in selfish and pleasurable pursuits, or by guilt and shame.

We often believe our shame is greater than that of others.

This belief is usually not true and comes under the heading of "terminal uniqueness."

These are a great excuse for isolating ourselves, wallowing in self-pity, or getting drunk or high.

Here, we need to remember that:

"We grow by our willingness to face and rectify errors and convert them into assets... Cling to the thought that, in God's hands, the dark past is the greatest possession you have - the key to life and happiness for others. With it you can avert death and misery for them." *(A.A. Page 124)*

We do this by transforming our self-centeredness into altruism, unselfish concern for the welfare of others.

In the process of turning our lives around, we begin to accept the good, bad, beautiful, and ugly parts of ourselves.

Without the bad and ugly, all we could do is judge.

With the bad and ugly we get to transform all our guilt and shame into great compassion because we *know*, from our own personal experience, what happens when *cravings* take control of a person's life.

We *understand*, from our own personal experience, how easy it is to *rationalize* lying, cheating, and stealing time or money from those who love and trust us.

We have *experienced* the hell of addiction.

We have been tortured and burned by the fires of anger, rage, resentments, self-hatred, loneliness, despair, self-pity, and boredom.

From these ashes, we can rise from the slavery of addiction and make a miraculous comeback.

We can learn how to tame the powerful forces that create so much pain and suffering in our lives and the lives of those we love, what Buddha called, *The Three Poisons: Delusional Thinking, Destructive Emotions, and Cravings.*

As we make this comeback, there is one thing we can count on. We will encounter many obstacles. These obstacles are there for a reason. They force us to reach deep inside ourselves and develop the qualities it takes to become an addiction survivor: Courage, honesty, humility, endurance, resilience, faith, and teamwork. It's how we build and strengthen our spiritual muscle.

One of the primary reasons A.A. has gone from a very high *recovery* rate to a very high *failure* rate is that we, unlike the original members of A. A, don't believe there are any **requirements** for becoming an addiction survivor.

Can you imagine telling an athlete there are no requirements for winning a gold medal at the Olympics?

Can you imagine telling someone diagnosed with cancer that there are no requirements for becoming a cancer survivor?

Can you imagine telling a naval cadet that there are no requirements for becoming a NAVY SEAL?

Perhaps this idea, that there are no requirements for becoming an addiction survivor, is the greatest obstacle to getting off the *Relapse Roller Coaster Ride.*

I believe that the reason we have such a tragic failure rate is that we ignore the experience, wisdom, and solution passed on to us by the original members of A.A.

REQUIREMENTS

1. "To get over drinking will **require** a transformation in thought and attitude." *(A.A. Page 143)*
2. "Belief in the power of God, plus enough willingness, honesty, and humility to establish and maintain the new order of things were the essential **requirements.**" *(A.A. Page 14)*
3. "In the face of collapse and despair, in the face of the total failure of their human resources, they found that a new power, peace, happiness, and sense of direction flowed into them. This happened soon after they

whole-heartedly met a few simple **requirements**." *(A.A. Page 50)*
4. "Almost none of us liked the self-searching, the leveling of our pride, the confession of our shortcomings which the process **requires** for its successful completion." *(A.A. Page 25)*
5. "Having made a personal inventory, what shall we do about it? ....This **requires** action on our part, which, when completed, will mean that we have admitted to God, to ourselves, and to another human being, the exact nature of our wrongs." *(A.A. Page 72)*
6. "Your candidate may give reasons why he need not follow all the program. He may rebel at the thought of a drastic housecleaning which **requires** discussion with other people." *(A.A. Page 94)*
7. "My friend suggested what then seemed a novel idea. He said, "Why don't you choose your own conception of God?.... It was only a matter of being willing to believe in a Power greater than myself. Nothing more was **required** of me to make my beginning." *(A.A. Page 12)*
8. How do we turn our will and our lives over to the care of God? "The first **requirement** is that we be convinced that any life run on self-will can hardly be a success." *(A.A. Page 60)*
9. "Burn the idea into the consciousness of every man that he can get well regardless of anyone. The only **condition** is that he trust in God and clean house." *(A.A. Page 98)*
10. "Unless each A.A. member follows to the best of their ability, our **suggested** Twelve Steps of recovery, they almost certainly sign their own death warrant." *(12 Steps and 12 Traditions, Page 174)*

Similarly, when you sky dive, it's **suggested** that you put on a parachute before leaving the plane.

Are you willing to meet the **requirements** for becoming an addiction survivor?

Are you willing to burn into your consciousness the **wisdom** passed on to us by the original members of A.A.?

Are you willing to **seek** a spiritual solution to your problem and go to any lengths to **find** a spiritual experience?

If you answered yes, then, congratulations!

Like Christopher Columbus, you will discover a new world, a world of intuition, imagination, creativity, and power.

In this new world, you will come to know and believe that you are *much more powerful* than your addiction, *much more powerful* than the obsessive thoughts, compulsive feelings, and physical cravings that have control and dominate your life.

In this new world, you will gain access to a Power that can transform your cravings for pills, alcohol, or drugs into cravings for courage, honesty, integrity, humility, and peace.

In this new world you will find:

A NEW FREEDOM

His friend told him very little
about the healing waters of the spa.
All he said was:

You will feel like a newborn child.
You will find a new freedom.
You must go.
He went.

Following the directions of the old man, he submerged his
body into
the hot, swirling waters of the spa.

As celestial music filled the air,
the old man said:
Close your eyes....
Until I tell you to open them.

His mind drifted.
Perfect peace, perfect tranquility.
He heard the old man's voice.
Open your eyes.

Panic set in.
He was surrounded by a dozen people.
People he had hurt in some way
during his life.

He wanted to hide.
But he was trapped.
No place to run.
He braced himself
for the battering
he was about to receive.

Each person,
looking deep inside his eyes
said:
I forgive you.
I love you.

Frozen tears of guilt and shame melted,
flowed down his cheeks,
like a spring mountain stream.

He felt lighter,
fifty pounds lighter.
He felt pure, innocent, clean,
like a newborn child.

The old man asked:
Do you want to experience
complete freedom?

He thought he had.
He felt forgiven, completely.
If there was more, he wanted it.
He nodded his response.

As the tears of guilt and shame continued to flow down his
cheeks, the old man said:
Close your eyes until I tell you to open them.

He felt it again, that perfect peace and tranquility.
He heard the old man's voice:
Open your eyes.

He felt the rage surge inside him.
To his left sat the father

who abandoned him.
To his right sat the child
who shamed him.

He asked the old man:
Why did you do this to me?

He replied:
*Because you said
You wanted to experience
complete freedom.*

Suddenly he knew
what he had to do
to be free.

Looking deep inside their eyes,
he said:

*I forgive you.
I love you.*

Bibliography

A.A. World Services, Inc. (1939) Alcoholics Anonymous, (1952) Twelve Steps and Twelve Traditions, (1967) As Bill Sees It

Anderson, Mac, (2008), Motivational Quotes, Simple Truths, LLC

Easwaran, (1990) Words To Live By, Blue Mountain Center For Meditation.

Ford, Debbie, (1990) Ten Essential Questions To An Extraordinary Life.

Kuhar, Michael, (2012) The Addicted Brain, FT Press

Lin, Derek, (2011) The Tao of Joy Every Day, Penguin Group

Meng--Dao, Dens, (1992), 365 Tao, Harper Collins

Powell, John S.J (1987), R L Benziger

Rohr, Richard, (2011) Breathing Under Water, Spirituality and the Twelve Steps, Saint Anthony Messenger Press

Twerski, Abraham, (1993) Seek Sobriety - Find Serenity, Pharos Books